YOUR FIRST YEAR AS A LAWYER
REVEALED

Secrets, Opportunities, and Success!

URSULA FURI-PERRY, JD

YOUR FIRST YEAR AS A LAWYER REVEALED: SECRETS, OPPORTUNITIES, AND SUCCESS!

© 2010 by Ursula Furi-Perry

Published by JIST Works, an imprint of JIST Publishing
7321 Shadeland Station, Suite 200
Indianapolis, Indiana 46256-3923

Phone: 800-648-JIST   Fax: 877-454-7839
E-mail: info@jist.com Web site: www.jist.com

Also by Ursula Furi-Perry: *Law School Revealed*

Quantity discounts are available for JIST products. Please call 800-648-JIST or visit www.jist.com for a free catalog and more information.

Visit www.jist.com for information on JIST, free job search information, tables of contents and sample pages, and ordering information on our many products.

Acquisitions Editor: Susan Pines
Development Editor: Stephanie Koutek
Cover Designer: Honeymoon Image and Design, Inc.
Interior Designer: Aleata Halbig
Interior Layout: Toi Davis
Indexer: Jeanne Clark

Printed in the United States of America

14 13 12 11 10 09   9 8 7 6 5 4 3 2 1

Library of Congress Cataloging-in-Publication Data
Furi-Perry, Ursula.
  Your first year as a lawyer revealed : secrets, opportunities, and success! /
by Ursula Furi-Perry.
       p. cm.
  Includes index.
  ISBN 978-1-59357-725-4 (alk. paper)
  1. Law--Vocational guidance--United States. I. Title.
  KF297.F873 2010
  340.023'73--dc22
                              2009045815

We have been careful to provide accurate information throughout this book, but it is possible that errors and omissions have been introduced. Please consider this in making any career plans or other important decisions. Trust your own judgment above all else and in all things.

ISBN 978-1-59357-725-4

GET AN INSIDER'S VIEW OF YOUR FIRST YEAR AS A LAWYER

Your First Year as a Lawyer Revealed includes valuable tips and information about achieving success during your first year on the job as a lawyer. The book offers valuable advice about getting your first job as a lawyer, succeeding on the job as a new lawyer, and thinking ahead in your legal career.

Your First Year as a Lawyer Revealed addresses various issues and topics that are important to today's recent law graduates and young lawyers: pinpointing your career interests, building marketable skills, increasing your productivity, networking, maintaining work-life balance, and finding the right fit.

Most importantly, *Your First Year as a Lawyer Revealed* contains valuable tips and advice from many sources who are familiar with legal careers and starting out as a new lawyer: career services professionals, law school administrators, law firm administrators, recruiters, experienced lawyers and other legal professionals, and young lawyers. For the graduating law student, the recent law graduate, the young lawyer, or anyone considering a career as a lawyer, *Your First Year as a Lawyer Revealed* offers a wealth of important information.

Acknowledgments

A heartfelt thank you to the entire JIST Publishing team for all of its hard work on this book. In particular, thank you to Sue Pines, Stephanie Koutek, and Selena Dehne.

Thanks also to the many wonderful career services professionals, law school administrators, law firm administrators, recruiters, lawyers, and other legal professionals who shared with me their insightful comments for this book. May your helpful advice be heeded by readers!

Thanks to the many law students, recent law grads, and colleagues who continue to inspire me and provide me with ideas and insights for new books.

As always, a big thanks to my family, particularly my husband, Tom, for all of his help and support.

Contents

INTRODUCTION   XV

PART I: GETTING YOUR FIRST JOB   1

CHAPTER 1: PINPOINTING YOUR CAREER INTERESTS   3

What Are Some of the Choices You'll
Have to Make When Starting Out
as a Young Lawyer?   3

What Factors Should You Consider
When Deciding on the Career Path
That's Right for You?   7

Weighing Your Options: A Self-
Assessment Worksheet for Law
Students and Recent Law Grads   10

Designing a Career Plan   22

A Sample Career Plan   27

Summation   29

Homework   30

CHAPTER 2: VARIOUS WORK ENVIRONMENTS FOR NEW
LAWYERS   31

Where Do New Lawyers Work?   32

Large-Firm Life   32

Small Firms   36

Self-Employment   41

Government and Public Interest Work   53

Other Career Options   54

Where Can You Find Firsthand
Accounts of What It's Like to Work
in a Particular Area?   56

Choosing the Work Environment
That's Best for You   58

Summation   64

Homework   65

CHAPTER 3: FINDING LEGAL EMPLOYMENT   **67**

Where the Jobs Are   67

Successful Strategies for the Job Hunt   70

What If You Can't Find Employment?   76

Summation   77

Homework   78

**CHAPTER 4: TIPS FOR CRAFTING YOUR RESUME AND
OTHER WRITTEN MATERIALS**   **79**

Resume Tips for Law Students and
Recent Law Grads   79

Writing a Great Cover Letter   83

Polishing Your Writing Sample   85

Letters of Recommendation and
References   87

Filling Out a Job Application and
Related Documents   89

Summation   90

Homework   91

**CHAPTER 5: PRESENTING YOURSELF TO A POTENTIAL
EMPLOYER**   **93**

Meeting a Potential Employer   93

Presenting Yourself to a Potential
Employer: Polishing Your
Professional Image   95

Crafting Your "Career Sound Bites"   98

Presenting a Professional Image
Online and Over E-mail   99

Summation 104

Homework 104

CHAPTER 6: INTERVIEWING TIPS **105**

What Does the On-Campus Interview
Process Entail? 105

What Questions Can You Expect
During OCI? 106

What Are Some Questions that You
Should Be Asking During
Interviews? 107

What Are Interviewers Looking For in
Candidates? 110

What Can You Expect During the
Call-Back Interview? 111

What Can You Expect at an Interview
with a Smaller Firm or Other
Employer? 113

How Can You Project a Professional
Image During the Interview? 114

Summation 115

Homework 116

**PART II: MAKING THE MOST OF YOUR
FIRST YEAR** **117**

CHAPTER 7: LEARNING ON THE JOB **119**

What Makes the First Year Potentially
the Most Difficult? 119

What Does "Training" Really Mean
When You're a New Lawyer? 122

What Are Some Opportunities for
Professional Development? 126

How Can You Find Great Mentors? 129

Questions to Ask Your Mentors 134

Summation 137

Homework 137

CHAPTER 8: GETTING MEANINGFUL ASSIGNMENTS 139

Getting Assignments: How Does It Work? 139

Ways to Show Your Abilities 141

Getting Evaluated and Conducting Self-Evaluations 145

Summation 148

Homework 149

CHAPTER 9: INCREASING YOUR MARKETABILITY AND BUILDING YOUR CLIENT BASE 151

What Must You Know About Making Yourself More Marketable? 151

Why Is It Essential for New Lawyers to Begin Building Their Books of Business as Soon as Possible? 154

Business Development Tips for Young Lawyers 156

Summation 159

Homework 159

CHAPTER 10: INCREASING YOUR PRODUCTIVITY—AND YOUR BILLING 161

Common Productivity Pitfalls—and Ways to Avoid Them 161

A Productivity Checklist: Pinpointing Your Productivity Strengths and Weaknesses 164

Billing Tips for Young Lawyers 165

Summation 166

Homework 166

Chapter 11: Building Your Network 169

What Does Networking Mean? 169

Networking Tips for the New Lawyer 171

Tips for Approaching Lawyers and
Legal Professionals (Even If You
Don't Know Them) 175

Summation 178

Homework 178

Chapter 12: Organizing Your Work and Your
Life, Managing Your Time, and Managing
Your Money 181

Tips for Honing Your Organizational
Skills 181

Time Management Tips for New
Lawyers 185

Managing Your Money 188

Technology Resources 191

Summation 193

Homework 194

Chapter 13: Ethics, Professionalism, Workplace
Etiquette, and Interacting with Others 197

An Ethics Primer for Young Lawyers 197

Tips for Avoiding Unprofessional
Conduct 199

The Ten Commandments of Ethics
and Professionalism for Young
Lawyers 200

Paying Attention to Diversity 204

Etiquette Tips on the Job 206

Tips for Interacting with Clients 208

Tips for Interacting with Partners and
Superiors 209

Interacting with Your Peers and Other
    Associates   211

Summation   212

Homework   213

CHAPTER 14: MAINTAINING WORK-LIFE BALANCE, PREVENTING BURNOUT, AND MANAGING YOUR STRESS LEVEL   **215**

Maintaining Work-Life Balance   215

Spotting the Signs of Burnout: A
    Self-Assessment Questionnaire   217

Performing Pro Bono Work   220

Managing Your Stress Level and
    Maintaining Your Sanity   221

Summation   226

Homework   226

PART III: THINKING AHEAD   **227**

CHAPTER 15: MAKING THEM WANT TO KEEP YOU   **229**

Summation   235

Homework   235

CHAPTER 16: PLANNING FOR YOUR NEXT JOB   **237**

Onward and Upward to Your
    Second Job   237

Eight Proactive Steps Toward
    Changing Your Career Path   240

Summation   244

Homework   244

CHAPTER 17: HELPFUL ONLINE RESOURCES FOR YOUNG LAWYERS   **245**

Job Searching   245

Information About Legal Employers
    and Legal Careers   246

Practical Information About Getting
Started in Law Practice   246

Continuing Legal Education and
Professional Development   247

Networking and Professional
Associations for Young Lawyers   247

Work-Life Balance and Maintaining
Your Health and Sanity   248

GLOSSARY   249

INDEX   255

INTRODUCTION

As they say, the first year of doing anything new is always the hardest.

Transitioning from law student to new lawyer comes with some serious challenges: from learning on the job to developing your professional network, and from presenting a professional image to planning for long-term career satisfaction. *Your First Year as a Lawyer Revealed* offers valuable advice to new lawyers about navigating the first year on the job, providing value to your employers, building your network and developing your client base, and planning beyond the first year.

Your First Year as a Lawyer Revealed is divided into three parts:

- Part I includes helpful information about finding and getting your first job; factors to consider in choosing an employer; tips on resumes, interviewing, and meeting potential employers; and information about different legal employers and environments.

- Part II focuses on succeeding on the job and making the most of your first year: learning on the job as a new lawyer; honing your practical skills; developing lasting professional relationships; interacting with clients, supervisors, peers, and others; getting meaningful assignments; balancing your work with the rest of your life; honing organizational and time-management skills; becoming more productive and efficient; and representing your firm well on and off the job.

- Part III offers tips and advice on providing value to a present or potential employer and planning beyond the first year, along with helpful resources for young lawyers.

There are several components in this book to help you navigate your first year as a lawyer:

- The bulleted checklists throughout the book help you determine what you need to know and consider about important topics you'll face as a new lawyer—from honing organizational skills to managing your time; from billing to building and developing your book of business.

- The "Homework" sections at the end of each chapter, as well as additional career worksheets in several chapters, are in place for you to contemplate and complete; they'll help you determine your own preferences, needs, plans, and goals.

- The "Revealed" sections offer tips, advice, and insights from young lawyers who have weathered the transition from student to attorney.

- The sections titled "The Answers—Revealed" contain information and answers to some of the most pressing questions that law students and new lawyers have, presented in a Q&A format.

Though you must customize your experience as a first-year associate according to your own needs, career goals, and plans, you don't have to do it alone! Let *Your First Year as a Lawyer Revealed* serve as a helpful and valuable guidebook for success on the job as a new lawyer—and beyond.

PART I

Getting Your
First Job

Chapter 1: Pinpointing Your Career Interests

Chapter 2: Various Work Environments for New
Lawyers

Chapter 3: Finding Legal Employment

Chapter 4: Tips for Crafting Your Resume and
Other Written Materials

Chapter 5: Presenting Yourself to a Potential
Employer

Chapter 6: Interviewing Tips

Pinpointing Your Career Interests

A law degree affords you many career choices. This chapter details some of them and offers tips for deciding what you want to do on your first job and beyond. The chapter also includes a self-assessment test designed for new law graduates.

What Are Some of the Choices You'll Have to Make When Starting Out as a Young Lawyer?

To me, the job search process for recent law graduates has three distinct components:

1. You must assess your own strengths and weaknesses, career goals, and interests.

2. You must assess what types of work environments and career options may be a good fit for your skill set.

3. You must have a clear and comprehensive career plan in place to help you begin your job search.

All of this soul-searching and job-searching comes with many choices. Your first choice—one you should make while you're still in law school—may be deciding on the type of work environment that best fits your needs, goals, skills, aptitudes, and interests. Are you interested in working for a large or midsize firm, for example (and do you have the grades and qualifications to get the job), or is a small firm or other employer a better fit for you?

You may also have some "practical" choices to make when considering a potential employer. For starters, most recent law graduates carry a staggering debt load, so salary considerations are important (although depending on your job and industry, you may be eligible for debt-reduction programs or income-based repayment). The location of your employer, the commute you'll have, your potential work schedule, and any skills you'll have to learn or hone to do the job are some other examples.

As a law student or recent grad, you may also begin thinking about the practice area(s) or substantive area(s) of law that interest you. For example, you may know that you are interested in intellectual property law, have the requisite technical/scientific and legal training to enter that field, and have planned to work in that field for years—if so, it will make sense for you to apply to boutique firms practicing intellectual property or large or midsize firms that have an intellectual property practice group.

New lawyers are best served when they become immersed in the practice area that interests them, says Lisa Terrizzi, career coach and consultant and chairperson of the Massachusetts Bar Association's Lawyers in Transition Committee. For some, it can be difficult to switch practice areas later on.

On the other hand, you may simply know that you're interested in litigation or in transactional work, but not specifically seeking a job in a precise practice area. It's not always necessary or important to have a practice area pegged as the one you'll enter upon graduation. Many law grads fall into a practice area after they begin working at a firm, many don't know what they want to do until years after they graduate, and many others manage to change practice areas or even careers after starting out in their first jobs, so you shouldn't necessarily feel like you're behind the ball just because you're not dead set on a particular practice area.

Do think about perspectives such as the temperament of the industry or practice area and the intellectual stimulation you may have, says Terrizzi. Some practice areas may not be the right fit for your temperament if you prefer to keep your emotions out of the workplace—I, for example, know that I would never want to practice family law or juvenile law, and therefore I don't!

Don't fall into the trap of wanting a job—any job—so badly upon graduation that you hear only what you want to hear about a particular employer, warns Paula Zimmer, Assistant Dean and Director of Career Services at Western New England School of Law. Make sure you're going into the position with your eyes open, and think of the long run.

As hard as it sounds, you'll also have to make some tough choices about your lifestyle and the balance you aim to strike between your work life and the rest of your life. As you search for your first job, you'll have to understand and recognize that some legal jobs—if not most of them—will require some pretty serious trade-offs when it comes to your available time outside of the job. If you're going to work as a litigation associate at a large law firm, you must understand that long hours and long work weeks will be an everyday part of the job. If you're striking out on your own, understand that building a firm or business from the ground up means you're really never off duty.

As part of your job search, you must assess what a potential position and employer will require of you in terms of time, effort, and performance; you must also assess what the potential position will mean for you in terms of work-life balance. Will you still have some time left to tend to your obligations outside of work—and simply to relax or do some of the things you enjoy? While you probably recognize that the first year on the job as a new lawyer calls for a diligent and grueling performance at work, you also must beware of burnout.

One important note: You don't have to view your first job as a be-all, end-all position. While it's great to find the perfect fit right out of law school, aiming for perfection may be unrealistic.

It's perfectly okay to take a starter job, says William Chamberlain, Assistant Dean and Clinical Assistant Professor of Law at the Center for Career Strategy and Advancement at Northwestern University School of Law. Take the job you can get, Chamberlain says, and use it to build valuable legal experience, which you can then take with you to the next position. To some extent, this may mean that even after you've evaluated various employers, using all of those factors that are important to you, you have to go with your gut and trust that you're picking a place that's the right fit for your first year, Chamberlain explains—for example, by deciding that the attorneys at one firm were more like you.

Think of your legal career as a long journey: You may make a few stops—or even many stops—along the way, and you'll pick up valuable knowledge as you go. Just be sure that with every job you take, you make the most of your experience and learn some skills that will help you on your journey. So, take on a first job that will help set you up for the job you'll really want down the line and the future you envision for yourself and your career, explains Jason Wu Trujillo, Senior Assistant Dean for Admissions and Financial Aid at the University of Virginia School of Law. If you do love your first job, of course, all the better!

What Factors Should You Consider When Deciding on the Career Path That's Right for You?

Career materials and books for law grads often urge grads to focus on and try to find the "right fit." But just what does the "right fit" mean, and what goes into finding it on your first job? Here are some factors to help you get started, along with some questions to ponder when contemplating each factor.

- Your interests. For example:

  - Do you want to perfect your skills in one specialty or practice area, or would you rather work in a variety of practice areas and avoid being pigeonholed?

  - Do you want to do litigation or transactional work?

  - Do you want to feel that you are helping your community or the greater good in your work—and is that factor sufficiently important to you that you may consider an employer other than a private law firm?

  - Do you enjoy working with many clients, or would you rather build relationships with fewer clients whom you serve more closely?

  - Do you want to practice law, to practice law in nontraditional ways, or to leave the practice of law?

  - Do you want to be given substantive and meaningful work assignments—and what do those labels mean to you in practice?

- Your on-the-job needs and preferences. Maybe you want to work with a diverse group of people; maybe you want in-depth training and plenty of opportunities for professional development; maybe you're seeking a close-knit work environment. For example, ask the following questions:

  - Do you want to work in an environment that makes you feel comfortable every day, or would you rather work in an environment that frequently gets you out of your comfort zone?

  - Do you want to work for an employer whose values match yours closely or at a place where many different viewpoints and values are represented?

  - Do you want to work with people who are a lot like you or with a diverse group at an employer that values cultural sensitivity and diversity in the workplace?

  - Do you want plenty of opportunities for professional development and continuing education?

  - Do you want clear opportunities for advancement, along with requirements for advancement that are clearly spelled out?

  - Do you want to work for an employer that provides networking opportunities or many opportunities for socializing with colleagues outside of work?

- Your future career goals—both immediate and long-term goals and plans. For example:

  - Do you want a position that you hope to hold just for the next few years or a long-term position?

  - Do you want to build a skill set that will readily translate into a variety of career options in the future—and what particular skills do you want to be able to hone on the job?

- Do you want to work for an employer that's amenable to organizational change and growth?

- To what extent are you looking for long-term growth potential in your first position?

- Do you want to participate in important decisions that happen in the workplace?

- Is partnership at this firm a part of your long-term career goals?

- Your own skills and aptitudes, the potential employer's preferences, and the likelihood of you being hired for the position. You may have your heart set on a prestigious (and hard-to-come-by) big firm position with a high-paying salary, but if your grades and other qualifications don't measure up, you likely won't be offered that job.

When applying for a position, take an honest look at what the position requires and what the employer is seeking in candidates. For example, ask these questions:

- Does your skill set match the skill set the employer requires?

- What are some skills that you need to develop before taking on the position that you're considering?

- What are some of your marketable skills that you can highlight to the employer?

- What is the employer likely looking for in a first-year associate?

- Practical considerations. From the employer's location to salary to work schedules, you also need to weigh practical factors that may influence your decision on a particular employer. For example:

- Do you want a high salary or simply want to receive compensation that is fair in relation to that of your peers?

- Do you want a workplace that embraces merit-based compensation and promotions?

- Do you want to attain reasonable work-life balance, want a flexible or alternative schedule, or want to work part time?

- Do you want manageable billable hour quotas and deadlines?

- Do you want a manageable commute?

- Do you want satisfactory fringe benefits? In addition, do you want job perks—from the company BlackBerry to paid lunches?

Weighing Your Options: A Self-Assessment Worksheet for Law Students and Recent Law Grads

I spoke at a career conference organized by the Massachusetts Bar Association and developed the following self-assessment worksheet. This worksheet is designed to get you to think about some of the factors you'll have to weigh when deciding what types of jobs to apply for after law school. Use it as a guide to determine your preferences, skills, aptitudes, needs, goals, and other considerations that matter to you.

There are no right or wrong answers to these questions—what matters is that you use the questions to help you begin thinking about what's important to you in your first position.

Section 1: Your Skills and Aptitudes

What were some of the law school courses in which you did well?

_____

_____

What practical, clinical, on-the-job, or internship experience do you have to offer a legal employer?

_____

_____

What life experiences do you have that may help you perform well on the job as a new attorney?

_____

_____

What are some compliments about your performance that you've received from employers, supervisors, colleagues, or professors?

_____

_____

(continued)

(continued)

What are some critiques or criticisms about your performance that you've received from employers, supervisors, colleagues, or professors?

_____

_____

What are some of your marketable skills—in other words, what skills do you have that will allow you to offer value to a potential employer?

_____

_____

What parts of your legal education have proven to be the most challenging for you?

_____

_____

What parts of your legal education have proven to be the most rewarding?

_____

_____

What makes you stand out from other job applicants?

_____

_____

In what ways do you work well with others, and what are some past examples in which you successfully collaborated with others?

_____

_____

In what ways do you work well independently, and what are some past examples where you successfully worked independently on a project?

_____

_____

What do you consider your greatest success(es) in your legal education or experience?

_____

_____

Section 2: Your Interests

On the job or in school, what are some of the tasks that you look forward to doing?

_____

_____

(continued)

(continued)

What are some of the tasks that you dread?

_____

_____

If you have legal experience, what substantive areas or subjects do you most enjoy working on?

_____

_____

If you're a recent grad, what substantive legal courses did you most enjoy in law school?

_____

_____

What areas of the law do you see yourself practicing in?

_____

_____

What areas of the law would you not consider practicing in?

_____

_____

Go back to basics: What made you go to law school and choose the legal profession?

_____

_____

What are some of your interests outside of the law?

_____

_____

Section 3: Your Future Goals

Where would you like your career to be in

One year?

_____

_____

Five years?

_____

_____

Ten years?

_____

_____

(continued)

(continued)

What are some things you'd like to accomplish in your career?

_____

_____

You're reading your "career obituary." What does it say?

_____

_____

What are some personal goals you'd like to accomplish?

_____

_____

Section 4: Your Current Needs and Practical Considerations

After looking at your monthly budget upon graduation, what is the minimum salary that you'll need to support yourself?

_____

_____

What is the ideal salary you would seek on your first job?

_____

_____

Do you have any scheduling or timing issues that would limit you to working only a certain set schedule?

_____

_____

To what extent does the location of your employer matter to you—do you need or want to live in a certain place, or are you comfortable with relocating?

_____

_____

Are there any other practical considerations that you need to mull over before taking on a job?

_____

_____

(continued)

(continued)

Section 5: Your Potential Employers

In what type of work environment do you work best—for example, do you thrive at a large employer or school where many others work, or do you prefer a smaller workplace where you have few co-workers?

_____

_____

Are you interested in practicing law—and if so, would you prefer to practice in a private setting, government, or nonprofit employment?

_____

_____

Are you interested in an alternative legal career or a non-legal position?

_____

_____

What do you look for in an employer's organizational culture?

_____

_____

To what extent are the following factors important to you? Rate them on a scale of 1 through 10, with 1 being not at all important and 10 being extremely important.

Employer diversity: _____

Associate retention: _____

Associate training and professional development: _____

Meaningful work assignments: _____

Being challenged on the job: _____

Finding a mentor: _____

Work-life balance: _____

Pay: _____

Contributing to the greater good on the job: _____

Briefly rank the importance that each of the foregoing factors has to you as you contemplate different employers, from most important to least important:

_____

_____

(continued)

(continued)

What do you have to offer to a potential employer in terms of fit—in other words, how will you prove to a potential employer that you may fit well into the firm or place of employment?

_____

_____

What does the "right fit" mean to you?

_____

_____

Self-Assessment Results

Now that you've spent considerable time assessing your strengths, weaknesses, needs, and goals, take some time to mull over the data you've just assembled. What do your answers indicate? What do your self-assessment results tell you about the potential sources of employment that may be right for you?

Ask yourself the following questions:

Work environments: Do my answers indicate a clear preference for any particular work environment, such as large firms, small firms, government employment, or public-interest work?

_____

_____

Practice areas: Do my answers indicate a clear preference for any particular practice area(s)?

_____

_____

Other careers: Do my answers indicate a clear preference for any alternative legal careers or even non-legal careers?

_____

_____

Jobs to steer clear of: Do my answers indicate any particular types of jobs to stay away from?

_____

_____

Jobs for which I may be a good fit: Do my answers indicate any marketable skills that would transfer well into a particular position?

_____

_____

Jobs for which I may not be a good fit: Do my answers indicate any personal or professional weaknesses that may cause me not to perform well at a particular job?

_____

_____

Designing a Career Plan

You've assessed your options and considered potential sources of employment—now it's time to create a career plan that you can put into action to help you find that all-important first position.

Designing a career plan isn't always easy, but having a concrete plan to follow is extremely important. Not only will a career plan give you a more clear picture of where you want your career to go in the future, but it will also allow you to pinpoint the skills and areas that you still need to hone and focus on.

Here's a checklist you may find useful when designing your career plan.

Immediate Plans

Immediate goal:

_____

_____

_____

Requirements for immediate goal:

_____

_____

_____

Marketable skills required:

_____

_____

_____

Steps to be taken towards implementing immediate plans:

- Plans for meeting requirements:

  _____

  _____

  _____

- Plans for seeking employment:

  _____

  _____

  _____

- Plans for networking:

  _____

  _____

  _____

(continued)

(continued)

- Five new things to learn in order to further immediate goals:

  _____

  _____

  _____

- Target completion dates:

  _____

  _____

  _____

Long-Term Career Plans

Long-term career goals:

_____

_____

_____

Requirements for long-term goals:

_____

_____

_____

Marketable skills required:

_____

_____

_____

Necessary steps towards long-term goals:

- Experience:

  _____

  _____

  _____

- Professional and skills development:

  _____

  _____

  _____

- Other steps:

  _____

  _____

  _____

(continued)

(continued)

Implementing long-term plans

- Plans for professional development:

  _____

  _____

  _____

- Plans for honing important skills:

  _____

  _____

  _____

- Plans for networking:

  _____

  _____

  _____

- Plans for any transitions that may be required:

  _____

  _____

  _____

A Sample Career Plan

Eve is a third-year law student who's interested in transactional law. Her favorite law school course was Real Property, and she did well in her Contracts, Conveyancing, and Drafting Contracts classes. Eve's career plan may look like this:

Immediate plans: To work in the real estate law field

- Immediate goal: To find a position as a first-year associate.

- Requirements for immediate goal: Finish Juris Doctor degree; pass state bar examination; possess strong analytical, writing, research, drafting, and people skills.

- Marketable skills: Strong drafting skills; strong academic record; internship and clinical experience representing low-income clients with housing issues.

- Current career/professional interests: transactional law.

- Implementing immediate plans

  - Plans for meeting requirements: I plan to receive my Juris Doctor degree in June and sit for the bar examination in July. I plan to spend three days per week this summer on an internship at a small general-practice firm, where I will seek out opportunities to hone my drafting, writing, and analytical skills.

  - Plans for seeking employment: Contact my law school's career services office for referrals; participate in formal interviewing; contact attorneys I know who may be seeking a new associate.

  - Plans for networking: Join a trade association for real estate attorneys; join other professional associations; join my state bar's young lawyers association/

committee; keep in regular contact with classmates, colleagues, and professional contacts; attend a seminar, social event, or other networking opportunity.

- Three new things to learn in order to further immediate goals: 1) How to fill out a HUD financing statement; 2) How to draft the documents necessary to conduct a proper real estate closing; 3) The basics of representing buyers and sellers of foreclosed properties.

- Target completion: December 1.

Long-term career plans

- Long-term career goals: To own my own law firm, focusing on real estate law.

- Requirements for long-term goals: Build experience working in real estate law; learn the ins and outs of real estate law and hone the skills required to represent clients in transactions from beginning to end; build up clientele; build up capital needed to establish my own business; build up professional contacts and relationships.

- Necessary steps towards long-term goals:

  - Experience: Work for a firm for five to ten years as a real estate attorney; find mentors who can impart wisdom about working in the real estate field and about founding my own law firm.

  - Professional and skills development: Engage in yearly continuing legal education by attending seminars, reading about changes in the law, and keeping up with the real estate field; seek out business development and marketing training.

- Other steps: Pay off student loans and other debts within five to seven years; save 25% of income for three to five years to put towards capital for funding the new law firm.

- Implementing long-term plans

  - Plans for professional development: Attend at least two CLE seminars per year—one focusing on business/marketing skills, and one focusing on developments in real estate law.

  - Plans for honing important skills: Focus on business development and maintaining client relationships; focus on substantive skills.

  - Plans for networking: Maintain client relationships; maintain professional ties, including at trade and bar associations; maintain close personal ties with colleagues and others.

  - Plans for any transitions that will be required: Business and marketing training; formal training on small business ownership; formal training on money and time management; formal training on human resources and management functions.

Summation

- Start thinking about your potential options of employment as early as possible.

- Remember that the job search process has three distinct components: First, you must assess your own strengths and weaknesses, career goals, and interests; second, you must assess what types of work environments and career options may be a good fit for your skill set; and third, you must have a clear and comprehensive career plan in place to help you begin your job search.

- Consider various factors when mulling over your career options, and aim to find the "right fit" for you.

- Think of your legal career as a long journey: Pick up valuable knowledge as you go, and with every job you take, make the most of your experience and learn some skills that will help you on your journey!

Homework

- Fill out the self-assessment worksheet in this chapter, focusing on your own interests, goals, needs, and career aspirations.

- Consult your law school's career services office, a career coach, or a consultant for other self-assessment tests that may prove valuable in helping you decide what types of work may be right for you.

- Using the career plan worksheet in this chapter, draft your career plan, listing both immediate and long-term career goals and plans.

CHAPTER 2

VARIOUS WORK
ENVIRONMENTS FOR NEW
LAWYERS

W here do you want to work? This is a crucial question to answer before you start your first job out of law school. In fact, one challenge facing young lawyers is deciding what they want to do after graduation: There are many different fields, environments, settings, and positions in which they may find themselves, explains Paula Nailon, Assistant Dean for Professional Development at the University of Arizona Rogers College of Law.

It's important that you explore your options. Whether you prefer a large firm, small firm, government or public interest employer, other legal employer, or non-legal alternative employer, finding out about different work environments for new lawyers is an essential part of the job search process.

Where Do New Lawyers Work?

Here are some statistics from *Trends in Graduate Employment*, a NALP bulletin published in July 2009 by the Association for Legal Career Professionals:

- The market for new law graduates in the classes of 1997 through 2008 was quite strong, with overall employment close to or above 89 percent since 1997 and increases over the prior year in 2005, 2006, and 2007.

- The 91.9 percent employment rate for the class of 2007 represented a 20-year high.

- More than half of employed graduates obtain their first job at a law firm.

- Small firms of two to ten lawyers have supplied relatively more jobs than any other size firm.

- Also of note is the growing proportion of jobs in either very small or large firms, which since 2000 have accounted for more than 70 percent of law firm jobs taken by new graduates.

- In 2008, 33 percent of new graduates who reported their employment in the NALP survey found employment in firms with two to ten attorneys, while 42.3 percent found employment in firms with more than 101 attorneys.

Large-Firm Life

What's it like to be a first-year associate at a large law firm? According to the American Lawyer 100 lists, large firms are defined as firms with 250 or more attorneys. So, if you're working for a large firm, you can clearly expect to meet many people. You can also expect—simply because of the amount of resources available at large firms as opposed to small firms—that a large firm may have more formal training and evaluation programs; more professional development resources; and more rigid hierarchies, pay scales, and systems for supervision in place for its new associates. Most large firms have offices in large metropolitan locations such as New York City; Washington, D.C.; and Los Angeles.

Many large firms have a rigid interview structure in place as well (see Chapter 6 for more information about the on-campus interview process) and may first hire summer associates—students entering their last year of law school—who will work for the firm during the summer and may then receive an offer of full-time employment upon graduation.

Summer associate programs at large law firms are typically organized, structured, well-oiled machines, describes Dana Levin, U.S. Director of Legal Recruiting at Reed Smith, LLP. Summer associates get a taste of what it's like to work for a large firm, though Levin says the assignments they are given aren't always the same as those they will handle as new lawyers.

Many large law firms are structured in similar ways: with well-defined structures and well-defined roles for attorneys at each "lock-step" within the firm's structure. Typically, you're more likely to find a set hierarchy in place at large firms. As an example, there may be

- A managing partner at the top, who oversees and manages the firm's operations and business

- Senior partners, who have been promoted to partnership and have been working at the firm for a set number of years

- Junior partners, who have been promoted to partnership but have not been at the firm for as long as the senior partners (note, however, that some large firms may use criteria other than length of employment to determine the distinction between junior and senior partners)

- Senior associates, who have not yet been promoted to partnership but have been at the firm for a set number of years

- Junior associates, who are young lawyers like you and have been working at the firm for a limited number of years

- Attorneys of counsel, contract attorneys, and other lawyers who are providing services to the firm on a part-time or as-needed basis

- Support staff, including paralegals, legal assistants, legal administrators, and others (note that at many large firms, there may be a separate hierarchy in place for support staff as well: for example, there may be different tiers to indicate paralegals' experience, and there may be legal staff managers who oversee the work of support staff)

When you're first hired, you should work to understand the hierarchies in place at your firm. Doing so will help you better navigate the organizational culture, understand who may help you with questions or concerns, understand the roles and contributions of different people at the firm, and navigate office politics.

A large firm may also be structured around various practice groups, or departments in which lawyers work in a particular practice area. A new associate may be assigned to one practice group and receive tasks and assignments only in that area, or he or she may be assigned to several practice groups and float between them, performing various assignments for each group.

Practice groups can be as varied as the topics in which you may have taken courses in law school, depending on the interests and services of the firm and its attorneys. As just a few examples, the firm may have

- A corporate practice group, which handles transactional work for corporate clients

- A litigation practice group, which handles litigation work from pretrial to trial matters

- A banking or financial management practice group, which serves clients in the financial field

- An intellectual property practice group, which assists clients with their patent, trademark, copyright, and trade secret matters

Each practice group may in turn be overseen by additional managers or directors, such as a practice group manager. So, if you're working for a large firm, it's not uncommon to expect that you may have to answer to several superiors: for instance, your supervising partner, your practice group manager, your managing partner, and your formal mentor at the firm.

What does that mean for a new lawyer? Well, it means you will have to ensure that you're meeting the expectations of all of your supervisors and that you know whom to turn to with different kinds of questions that may arise.

REVEALED!

"[The most rewarding part of my job?] Generally, just helping my clients. Specifically, helping people achieve peace of mind knowing that they, themselves, are taken care of in case of an unexpected accident, knowing that their loved ones are also taken care of if there is disability or unexpected passing, and knowing that their hard-earned money is going to their loved ones in a thoughtful way with the least amount of transfer taxes."

Amir Atashi Rang, principal of The Atashi Rang Law Firm and 2000 UC Hastings graduate

Small Firms

When you're starting out at a small firm, your experiences will drastically differ from those of your peers who have opted to work for a larger firm. For starters, small firms typically lack the strict lock-step structure that most large firms employ; instead, the firm may simply have "associates" and "partners" and various support staff.

In addition, smaller firms may be more likely to expect new lawyers to be a "jack-of-all-trades" when it comes to handling new cases: Instead of being assigned much of the same types of tasks or projects, a new associate may be expected to handle all aspects of a case from beginning to end. You may also expect less in terms of "perks" and resources: While larger firms have the resources in place to formally train and oversee new associates, a smaller firm will more likely expect its new associates to hit the ground running, so to speak.

The practice areas in which you concentrate can also vary depending on the size of your employer. Some smaller firms (also known as "boutique firms") will specialize in just one practice area, and may even devote their practice to a subset of a particular practice area—for example, a boutique intellectual property firm may concentrate on patent prosecution and copyright applications. By contrast, some small firms (and even sole practitioners) may be generalists: They may accept cases from various different practice areas, such as criminal law, estate planning, family law, and real estate.

There are several skills that can help you if you are interested in working at a smaller firm. For starters, being quick on your feet, quick to learn, and able to quickly adapt to changing circumstances is essential at all firms, but especially at smaller firms where you may be expected to pull your weight very early on—both in terms of handling cases and matters and in terms of bringing in new business to the firm.

You'll greatly benefit from honing your business development skills if you're planning on joining a small firm. In addition, the more practical skills and practical experience you develop before going on board, the more likely you'll adapt to a small firm's fast-paced environment, which will require you to quickly take charge of your own cases, projects, and clients.

Working for a small firm or as a solo practitioner often means less access to on-site resources—and that means you'll have to get those resources on your own. Consider the vast array of resources offered by the American Bar Association's General Practice, Solo & Small Firm Division at http://new.abanet.org/divisions/genpractice/Pages/Resources.aspx.

Business of Law

- Cost Recovery: A variety of documents and information to help you determine whether you can recover costs. http://www.abanet.org/genpractice/resources/costrecovery/index.html

- Start and Run a Law Firm: Information on the business of law for both experienced solo and small-firm attorneys and those just starting out. http://www.abanet.org/genpractice/resources/startafirm.html

- Technology: General technology links, including e-mail lists, podcasts, articles, and more. http://www.abanet.org/genpractice/resources/tech.html

- Blogs: Information about what blogs are and how to start one; listings of good legal blogs, including blogs to help you run your practice. http://www.abanet.org/genpractice/resources/blawgs.html

- Cool Tools: A collection of useful and free tools online, including social bookmarking, feedreaders, photo tools, calendars, and much more. http://www.abanet.org/genpractice/resources/cooltools.html

- Web Site Development: Information to help you start your own Web site, from how to do HTML to search engine optimization. http://www.abanet.org/genpractice/resources/website.html

- Insurance: Information on malpractice insurance and several offerings to solo and small-firm ABA members through the American Bar Endowment. http://www.abanet.org/genpractice/resources/insurance.html

- Quality of Life: A collection of work-life balance resources and fun links, including timewasters, humor, music, health, and much more. http://www.abanet.org/genpractice/resources/life.html

Resources for Groups

- Diversity: http://new.abanet.org/divisions/genpractice/Pages/diversity.aspx
- Law students: http://new.abanet.org/divisions/genpractice/Pages/lawstudents.aspx
- Military lawyers: http://new.abanet.org/divisions/genpractice/Pages/military.aspx
- Young lawyers: http://new.abanet.org/divisions/genpractice/Pages/younglawyers.aspx
- Visit the Committee page for a full listing of substantive committees based on practice area and setting. http://new.abanet.org/divisions/genpractice/Pages/Committees.aspx

Practice of Law

- The Practice Areas page has links to select sites focused on practice areas. http://www.abanet.org/genpractice/resources/practiceareas.html
- Visit the Research page for resources to help you with both legal research and general research. http://www.abanet.org/genpractice/resources/research.html

(continued)

(continued)

Alternative Dispute Resolution

- The National Arbitration Forum (NAF) is a leading provider of out-of-court alternative dispute resolution solutions, including arbitration and mediation. NAF provides solutions for solo and small-firm practitioners and their clients in all 50 states and 28 countries. NAF's 1,500 legal experts resolve cases by applying the substantive law, offering litigants the same outcomes as court, but at much less time and cost.

- ABA Section of Dispute Resolution.

- Cornell University Institute on Conflict Resolution.

- ADR Resources.

Pro Bono/Low Bono and Public Service

- The Tolerance Through Education Project: This national public service project recruits lawyers to visit third-grade classrooms to help children appreciate diversity.

- The ABA Division for Public Education provides everything lawyers need to help educate students and the general public about the law.

- The ABA Standing Committee on Pro Bono and Public Service is the resource for information on pro bono.

- The Commission on the Renaissance of Idealism in the Legal Profession has created the *Pro Bono and Public Service Best Practice Resource Guide* to help lawyers learn from others' experiences and submit their own for others' benefit.

- The Law School Consortium Project provides support and service to solo and small-firm practitioners who are committed to serving low- and moderate-income individuals and communities.

Self-Employment

Although doing so is generally discouraged by experienced attorneys, some new lawyers start out working for themselves—as sole practitioners who work alone or as lawyers who found their own law firms by partnering with other lawyers.

Self-employment can certainly have many rewards: You can customize your own work schedule and potentially (though not always in practice) work as much or as little as you want; you can have more autonomy over the cases, clients, projects, and work assignments you take on; and you get to keep the profits you earn from your work.

Still, solo practice is not for everyone, and it can be exponentially difficult to engage in when you're a new lawyer with no experience under your belt. As a new grad, you have not developed a book of business, and you may find it difficult to line up clients and cases, at least as you get started.

Plus, because most new lawyers graduate with no (or precious little) practical experience, it can be hard to take on new cases and be thrown into the practice of law without having an established firm or at least a full-time supervisor behind you. Think carefully before you decide to hang your shingle. To determine whether self-employment may be a good fit for you, consider the following worksheet.

Worksheet: What Questions Should You Consider Before Hanging Your Shingle?

Setting Up Shop

What type of business organization makes sense for your firm—for example, should you incorporate as a professional corporation, operate as a partnership, or consider another kind of organizational structure?

_____

_____

What liability issues do you need to consider?

_____

_____

_____

Do you have a clear and comprehensive business plan in place?

_____

Will you be going into business alone or with partners (and what are the implications of your choice)?

_____

_____

_____

_____

Your Initial Business Needs

What type of office space or workspace will you need?

_____

_____

_____

_____

What equipment and furniture will you need to buy or lease?

_____

_____

_____

_____

(continued)

(continued)

What utilities will you need to have in place (such as a phone line, Internet connection, and electricity) in order to get started?

_____

_____

_____

_____

What other supplies will you need?

_____

_____

_____

What services and help will you be needing from other professionals—for example, will you need CPA services? The help of an information technology specialist? A subscription to a legal research database?

_____

_____

_____

_____

Will you need to hire support staff on a full-time or part-time basis?

_____

_____

_____

_____

Can you share any of your expenses (such as your office space or even your support staff) with another lawyer?

_____

_____

_____

_____

Budgeting and Finances

What does your overall budget look like, and how much will you need to earn in order to stay afloat?

_____

_____

_____

_____

(continued)

(continued)

Do you have a sufficient amount of money set aside to finance the business? (A good rule of thumb: You should have a good portion of an entire year's worth of expenses set aside before you get started, as it can take up to a year for a new firm to begin drawing profits.)

_____

Do you have a clear and comprehensive written budget and financial plan in place?

_____

Have you set up a precise and secure system for tracking expenses and income?

_____

What types of bank accounts (including client fund accounts) do you need to open?

_____

_____

_____

_____

What types of insurance (including liability or malpractice insurance) do you need to purchase?

_____

_____

_____

_____

Your Practice

What practice areas or fields will you focus on in your practice?

_____

_____

_____

_____

What types of cases will you accept?

_____

_____

_____

What types of cases will you definitely not accept?

_____

_____

_____

_____

(continued)

(continued)

Do you have a clear and comprehensive list of services that you will offer to your clients?

_____

What will make your practice unique? In other words, what will differentiate your practice from other firms?

_____

_____

_____

Clients and Business Development

Who are your future clients—your target market?

_____

_____

_____

_____

Do you have a ready-built client base (perhaps from a former job, in your personal network, or in your community) to whom you can advertise your services?

_____

Do you have a potential client base that you can tap?

_____

Advertising and Marketing

What types of traditional and nontraditional advertising will you engage in?

_____

_____

_____

_____

What types of online marketing will help you get started?

_____

_____

_____

_____

Do you have a formal marketing plan in place?

_____

_____

(continued)

(continued)

_____

_____

Whom can you call in your professional and personal network to help you get the word out about your services?

_____

_____

_____

_____

Professional Development, Help, and Feedback

What plans do you have for continuing legal education and periodic professional development?

_____

_____

_____

_____

What plans do you have for client evaluations of your services and for periodic self-evaluations?

_____

_____

_____

_____

Who are some trusted mentors to whom you can turn with questions?

_____

_____

_____

_____

List any experienced attorneys whom you can call when you encounter something you need guidance with while working on a case or project.

_____

_____

_____

_____

(continued)

(continued)

Are you sufficiently comfortable working on your own as a new attorney?

_____

What are the practical skills and areas you still need to hone in order to best serve your clients?

_____

_____

_____

_____

Are you fully informed about the rules of ethics and professional responsibility that govern the conduct of attorneys in your jurisdiction?

_____

List any sole practitioners or self-employed attorneys whom you may call on for advice about setting up your own law firm.

_____

_____

_____

_____

Government and Public Interest Work

Many law graduates are interested in working for the government or working in a public service or social justice position. Some examples of employers that hire new lawyers include

- District attorneys' and prosecutors' offices

- Public defenders' offices

- U.S. Attorneys' offices

- The U.S. government, including plenty of positions in administrative law, from education law to environmental and natural resources regulation and from energy law to antitrust and trade regulation

- Local and municipal governments

- The military

Check out the many resources offered by the American Bar Association's Government and Public Sector Division at http://www.abanet.org/govpub/sites.html.

Sites of Interest

- CapitolHearings.org: C-SPAN's schedule of Congressional hearings. http://www.capitolhearings.org/

- U.S. Government Index: Research and reference concerning U.S. government agencies, policies and laws. http://www.linxnet.com/gov.html

(continued)

(continued)

- Public Service JobNet: Government and public interest job listings produced by the Office of Public Service of the University of Michigan Law School. http://cgi2.www.law.umich.edu/_JobNet/

- E-Journal Finder: Georgetown University Law Library's online search tool for electronic journals, periodicals, and newspapers. http://www11.tdnet.com/Frames.asp

- Prosecuting Attorneys, District Attorneys, Attorneys General, and U.S. Attorneys on the Web: A listing of more than 3,000 Web sites compiled by the Eaton County, Michigan, Prosecuting Attorney's Office. http://www.eatoncounty.org/Departments/ProsecutingAttorney/ProsList.htm

- A–Z Index of U.S. Government Departments and Agencies: Comprehensive list of Web sites for federal government departments and agencies. http://www.firstgov.gov/Agencies/Federal/All_Agencies/index.shtml

- State Statutes and Legislation on the Web: Links to full-text state statutes. http://www.prairienet.org/~scruffy/f.htm

Other Career Options

There are other career options for new law grads, whether they be practicing positions outside of firms, alternative legal positions, or positions that are entirely outside of the legal field.

The Juris Doctor is an incredibly versatile degree—new law grads come out of law school with specialized and valuable training in analytical thinking, writing, and communication skills, all of which are valued by legal and non-legal employers alike.

The following are some examples of career options to consider:

- Some lawyers work at corporate law departments in various capacities. There they serve corporations as in-house counsel, taking care of the company's legal needs from transactions to mergers to due diligence.

- Legal aid and public interest positions present another career path for new JDs. From nonprofit organizations to public defenders' offices to legal aid offices that assist low-income clients, public interest–minded JDs have plenty of options.

- A small percentage of lawyers are employed in academia or teaching careers. These include law school faculty and administration, but JDs also find jobs teaching at colleges and universities and even primary and secondary schools.

- Some lawyers work in nontraditional legal careers. For example, some JDs found businesses that offer legal services to other attorneys, such as trial preparation services, legal research and writing services, and marketing services. Other JDs work in law office administration, handling the business side of the practice of law.

- Some lawyers work for the courts as judges, magistrates, or clerks or in other positions. New law graduates also have an opportunity to do a judicial clerkship. These are prestigious positions working for a court or an individual judge, where new JDs assist with legal research, writing, and other tasks. Judicial clerkships are often term-limited, and they are very competitive, usually going to top law students.

If you're interested in a clerkship, do your research about different courts' requirements and plan to submit your application early in your last year of law school.

- And finally, some lawyers shun the legal profession altogether and instead put their JDs to use in non-legal careers. From banking to business, many employers appreciate the skill set that JDs bring to the table.

Where Can You Find Firsthand Accounts of What It's Like to Work in a Particular Area?

Interested in a particular career option and want to learn more? Law students and recent graduates can find valuable information by reading firsthand accounts from young lawyers working in a particular area or at a particular firm. The following are some of my favorite resources:

- Vault.com has a yearly survey in which associates rank their own law firms on various factors (and dish about what it's like to work for them). See www.vault.com.

- The National Association for Legal Career Professionals offers many resources on working in various practice areas. See www.nalp.org.

- The *National Jurist* frequently profiles young lawyers who work in a particular practice area. See www. nationaljurist.com.

- Building a Better Legal Profession offers a *Guide to Law Firms* that's specifically geared towards law students and recent law grads trying to find information on working for various law firms. See www.betterlegalprofession.org.

- The National Association of Women Lawyers ranks law firms on their retention and promotion of women lawyers. See www.nawl.org.

Finally, you can also spend time with an attorney who works in a practice area or work environment that interests you. Take an attorney to lunch or coffee and pick his or her brain about the attorney's work. Alternatively, call a law firm or attorney acquaintance—or someone to whom you're referred by another person you know—and request a formal informational interview, where you seek to find out information about working in the attorney's field or practice area.

During the informational interview or your informal meeting with the attorney, you may start by asking the attorney the following nine questions:

1. What are your job duties and responsibilities?

2. What is the typical day (or week or month) like on the job?

3. Please describe how you obtained your current position, and please briefly describe the journey that took you to it.

4. What skills and characteristics do you possess that help you do well in your job every day?

5. What are the greatest challenges that you encounter on the job?

6. What do you consider the most rewarding parts of your job?

7. What surprised you most when you first started out in your field?

8. What tips and advice could you share with me about working in your field?

9. What general advice would you offer to a new attorney about the first year on the job?

Use these questions as a starting point. When the interviewee tells you something important or something that interests you, ask pointed follow-up questions. Customize the interview so that you find out about the information that is most pressing to you personally.

Choosing the Work Environment That's Best for You

As I've continually said, the Juris Doctor is one very versatile degree that's appreciated by employers in many different fields and environments. As you can see from the information in this chapter, this means law graduates have a plethora of different types of employers to choose from.

Is your head spinning yet about how you're supposed to make that choice? In my book, *50 Unique Legal Paths* (ABA Publishing, 2009), I pinpoint the following 100 factors for you to mull over:

1. I want to enjoy my work.

2. I want to work in a position where I have the power to help others.

3. I want to work on something new every day.

4. I want my job to challenge me.

5. I want a job that will use me to my fullest potential.

6. I want to learn something new every day.

7. I want to feel that I am helping my community in my work.

8. I want to perfect my skills in one specialty or practice area.

9. I want to work in various practice areas; I don't want to be pigeon-holed.

10. I want to feel confident about my work product.

11. I want a satisfactory salary.

12. I want satisfactory fringe benefits.

13. I want to receive compensation that is fair in relation to that of my peers.

14. I want a workplace that embraces merit-based compensation and promotions.

15. I want job perks—from the company BlackBerry to paid lunches.

16. I want to attain reasonable work-life balance, including time for my family, personal pursuits, and hobbies.

17. I want manageable billable-hour quotas.

18. I want manageable deadlines.

19. I want to have a flexible or alternative schedule.

20. I want to be able to work part-time if I choose.

21. I want to work in a field that offers assistance with student loan repayment.

22. I want to work for an employer that doesn't pressure its attorneys to bring in new business.

23. I want to work for an employer that encourages its attorneys to bring in new business.

24. I want to work for an employer whose values match mine closely.

25. I want to work at a place where many different viewpoints and values are represented.

26. I want to work with colleagues who have a strong work ethic.

27. I want to work in an environment that makes me feel comfortable every day.

28. I want to work in an environment that frequently gets me out of my comfort zone.

29. I want plenty of opportunities for advancement.

30. I want plenty of opportunities for professional development and continuing education.

31. I want plenty of opportunities to perform pro bono work.

32. I want to work for an employer with low attrition rates.

33. I want to have access to cutting-edge legal technology and resources.

34. I want to have access to an advanced law library.

35. I want a pleasant work environment, up-to-date facilities, and positive working conditions.

36. I want to have access to help by support staff.

37. I want to work with a diverse group.

38. I want to work with people who are a lot like me.

39. I want to work for an employer that values cultural sensitivity and diversity in the workplace.

40. I want to be in court a lot.

41. I want to write a lot.

42. I want to research a lot.

43. I want to have lots of client contact.

44. I want to enjoy working with the clients I serve.

45. I want to negotiate with others.

46. I want to help others resolve their controversies.

47. I want the opportunity to attend plenty of networking functions.

48. I want to work for an employer that provides opportunities for socializing with colleagues outside of work.

49. I want to work for a large firm.

50. I want to work for a small firm.

51. I want to work for the government.

52. I want to work for a nonprofit organization.

53. I want to work in education or academia.

54. I want to be my own boss.

55. I want recognition for my contributions at work.

56. I want to be busy at work.

57. I want to feel productive at all times.

58. I don't want to feel overwhelmed by the amount of work I am given.

59. I want to practice law.

60. I don't want to practice law.

61. I want to practice law in nontraditional ways.

62. I want to have the opportunity to train or teach others in my areas of expertise.

63. I want to be given authority over my own cases.

64. I want to be given substantive and meaningful work assignments.

65. I want the opportunity to travel for work.

66. I want the opportunity to work with people from other countries or cultures.

67. I want to be involved in the day-to-day operations and management of my workplace.

68. I want my own office.

69. I want to have periodic evaluations and frequent feedback.

70. I want to have clearly defined and explained performance goals set for me by my workplace.

71. I want firmly defined company policies in place, communicated clearly to me and other employees.

72. I want to know that I have supervisors to whom I can turn with questions.

73. I don't want to be micro-managed.

74. I want access to formal and informal mentoring on the job.

75. I want a workplace with an "open door" policy, where my supervisors and colleagues are approachable.

76. I want a workplace where the channels of communication are open.

77. I want to work with partners or senior-level staff as closely as possible.

78. I want to have collegial respect for my co-workers, including my supervisors.

79. I want to experience collegial respect from my co-workers, including my supervisors.

80. I want to make friends with my co-workers.

81. I want to be left alone to work independently.

82. I want a workplace where office politics are kept to a minimum.

83. I want to have colleagues who exhibit a high level of professionalism.

84. I want to work for an employer that has a positive reputation in the legal and business communities.

85. I want to work for an employer that has an international presence.

86. I want a workplace that is loyal to its employees and whose employees likewise exhibit loyalty to the firm.

87. I want a workplace that is well-managed.

88. I want a workplace with a proven record of profitability.

89. I want to work for a prestigious employer.

90. I want a workplace that pays attention to marketing its attorneys and legal services.

91. I want to build a skill set that will readily translate into a variety of career options in the future.

92. I want to work in a position that will ultimately advance not only my skill set, but also my long-term career goals.

93. I want an entry-level position that I hope to hold just for the next few years.

94. I want a long-term position.

95. I want a manageable commute.

96. I want to share in the profits that my employer derives from my work.

97. I want job security.

98. I want to participate in important decisions that happen in my workplace.

99. I want to work for an employer that's amenable to organizational change and growth.

100. I want to feel proud of the work I do.

Summation

- Research and carefully explore the many different environments, career options, and potential positions available to new law graduates.

- Whether you're interested in large-firm work, small-firm employment, self-employment, government or public interest work, or another career option, familiarize yourself with your chosen option. In particular, find out the answers to these questions:

  - What does the job entail?

  - What typical tasks and projects do new associates in that position or work environment handle?

  - What do other young lawyers say about working in that position?

- What can a new lawyer expect when working in that position?

- How does one get hired and started in the position?

- Remember that the Juris Doctor is an incredibly versatile degree that offers many different career options!

Homework

- Pinpoint three to five career options that interest you (use the self-assessment worksheet you completed in Chapter 1 for help). Do some research on each of the options you came up with: What does the job entail? What is it like to work in that field? How does one get started in the field?

- Conduct an informational interview with a person who works in a job or practice area that interests you. Use the worksheet earlier in this chapter to get started and then ask follow-up questions about information you'd like to obtain or points you'd like the interviewee to elaborate on.

- Spend some time thinking about the 100 factors you should consider regarding potential sources of employment. Write down ten to twenty "must-haves": factors that are very important for you to find in an employer. Then, write down ten to twenty factors that you'd like to find in a potential employer but are willing to compromise on—factors that won't make or break your decision when it comes to choosing the right fit. Finally, jot down five to ten factors that are absolutely not important to you—those that you can definitely live without.

CHAPTER 3

FINDING LEGAL EMPLOYMENT

W hether you're interested in Big Law or small firms, this chapter describes where the jobs are — and how to find them.

Where the Jobs Are

There are many ways to find a legal job. Some law firms hire primarily through formal interviewing processes, while others find their potential employees almost exclusively through networking. As a recent law graduate, you must keep your eyes — and your options — open when looking for your first job. Consider the following methods for finding employment.

Formal On-Campus Interviewing

Some firms — particularly larger ones — have a formal interview process in place that they follow when considering potential applicants. Your law school may participate in the on-campus interview process (described in more detail in Chapter 6) or may hold job fairs or similar programs at which employers engage in the formal interviewing of applicants. If your school participates in formal interview programs, you should take advantage of them.

Remember to sign up early—many employers with formal programs also have a regimented schedule for conducting interviews—and check on any requirements the employer or the school/hosting organization may have in place for applicants to participate in the process.

Online and Print Resources

Although it's increasingly tough to get a job by simply clicking a button and submitting a resume, job search engines online and job postings online and in print can still provide you with some potential leads in your job search.

For some candidates, that great first job comes in the form of an ad—a job posting online or in a print publication. Here are some of my favorite Web sites and publications to check for job leads:

- LawCrossing.com, www.lawcrossing.com
- Martindale-Hubbell, www.martindale.com
- Monster.com, www.monster.com
- Hotjobs.com, www.hotjobs.com
- Robert Half Legal, www.roberthalflegal.com
- Lawyers Weekly Jobs, www.lawyersweeklyjobs.com
- Craigslist, www.craigslist.org (choose your location and then click on the "legal/paralegal" category in the "jobs" section)
- Your local *Lawyers' Weekly* or comparable trade publication

- Your state and local bar association's trade journals, newsletters, and other publications

- Specialty bar associations' trade journals, newsletters, and other publications

- Your law school's job board or references to job postings online or in print

Informal Job-Finding and Networking

Don't let the above title fool you: "Informal" job searches and networking are just as important as—and perhaps more important than—any formal process or online job search you could sign up for, and they actually account for the majority of successful job searches out there.

In fact, networking is such an integral component of finding a job that some experts recommend that job seekers spend as much as 60 percent of their time on in-person networking, with 30 percent of their time spent on phone and e-mail connections and just 10 percent of their time spent on blind submissions and applying for formally posted job openings.

How do you get started? Consider the following sources for your job search:

- Your law school's career services office

- Your law school and your college alumni associations

- Professors, supervisors, or others who have overseen your work in the past

- Attorneys who are familiar with you or your work

- People in your community who may know of lawyers and firms that are hiring

- Your professional network, your friends, and your family

REVEALED!

"I believe that if you are working for a cause that you are passionate about and interested in, it will be the "right fit." A good working environment (supervisors, peers, etc.) also helps! I chose a career (teaching and solo practitioner) that fit my goals and interests, and also allowed a great deal of professional flexibility.... Think outside the box and don't be afraid to create a position for yourself if you cannot find what you are looking for."

Christie Edwards, asylum attorney and adjunct professor; 2007 Thomas Jefferson School of Law graduate

Successful Strategies for the Job Hunt

- Do your research before you hit "send." Make sure you understand who the employer is, what job you are applying for, what the qualifications are for the position, and what the job entails. Different firms and other legal employers employ different titles for various positions— for example, the title "clerk" may call for a very different skill set depending on the potential employer. Be clear about what the job entails.

- Familiarize yourself with any specific requirements the employer has in place before you apply for the position. For example, federal government jobs call for a very specific test based on applicants' knowledge, skills, and aptitude. Be sure you understand and comply with any special requirements the employer has set for job applicants.

- Customize your resume, cover letter, and communications to every position you apply to—one big mistake job seekers make is sending out the same generic resume and cover letter to every potential employer. Show the employer that you not only understand the specific position's requirements but also are the right fit for the position, highlighting your unique set of skills on each application, cover letter, or copy of your resume.

- Keep close track of your job search and document everything you do. Come up with an organized system for tracking every contact, follow-up, application, and communication with a potential employer. For example, list

  - The date you applied for a new job

  - The materials you sent or brought with you as part of your application

  - The date you followed up on a job application

  - Any communications you received from the employer in response to your application or follow-up

  - The date you made contact with a potential employer

  - The substance of your communication with the employer

  - Any referrals you received as part of that communication

  - Any job offers you receive, with detailed information about the position and your response to the employer

- Always be prepared to meet with a potential employer. Keep contact information with you and aim to project a professional image at all times.

- Join a professional association. You'll keep up with news and trends in your profession, get the chance to attend continuing legal education and professional and social events, meet others in your field, and get the opportunity to network. Plus, many professional associations maintain their own job boards, job listings, and other career resources for members.

- Get your foot in the door. Plenty of people started out in a legal position they considered a springboard to another legal career.

- Observe professional etiquette when it comes to job applications, communicating with potential employers and others, and dealing with job offers. If you receive an offer and you aren't sure as to whether you'll accept (or you're still waiting to hear back from other employers on their potential offers), be sure you let the employer know how much time you'd like before you make your decision.

  Also be prepared to say no to a job offer that isn't right for you—this may not seem like an easy thing to do just out of law school, but ultimately, you are better off going with a position that will be the right fit.

- Invest in professional development: Enroll in continuing legal education courses, attend a trade event, or take in a "webinar" in your field. You'll learn substantive law or practical tips that will help you on the job, plus you'll network with other professionals—and one of them may just know of a position that's perfect for you! In addition, continuing professional development looks great on a resume.

- Ask the career office at your law school or paralegal program for assistance.

- Consider nontraditional legal employers. Interested in practicing criminal law, for example? Don't just send your resume to criminal defense firms; check out career options in prosecution, public defense, or other social justice employers.

- Be proactive about your job search, stresses Charles Volkert, Chief Executive Officer of the Robert Half Legal international recruiting agency. Remember that there are many first-year associates on the market—you must, therefore, differentiate yourself from the pack based on your positive qualities. Just waiting for the right job to find you won't be enough.

   Be flexible, Volkert stresses: Even if some of the opportunities you really want are not available to you right off the bat, consider alternative sources of employment and keep an open mind.

   As an example, Volkert says some first-year associates who can't get full-time employment right out of law school turn to temporary or project-based employment, which allows them to build their networks while getting some legal experience rather than just sitting at home waiting for the "right" full-time job to show up.

- Don't be afraid to do some "targeted cold-calling." Volkert says one mistake that young lawyers make is in sending an impersonal resume only to the contact who's listed on a job posting—without any personal connection. Volkert instead recommends targeting particular partners at the firm with whom you may have something in common, such as a shared alma mater or having served on the same professional association.

- Align yourself with a trusted partner who can help you pinpoint potential leads that may be a good fit for your skill set. A career coach or counselor or a recruiter who specializes in the legal field may be able to offer you valuable insights and advice and introduce you to potential employers who are hiring.

- Don't discount yourself. One of the biggest mistakes job applicants make is not applying for a position at all. Remember: You can't get the job if you don't try for it!

- Don't exaggerate on your resume, cover letter, or any other communication with a potential employer—be sure that everything you send or say to an employer is truthful.

- Also remember to stay positive during your job search. Looking for a job can take months (even a year or more), which is obviously frustrating for the new JD with loads of debt. Still, you must approach the job search the same way that you would approach your new position: with energy, enthusiasm, and a positive attitude.

THE ANSWERS—REVEALED!

Q: What tips do you have for finding a job during meager economic times?

A: Times are tough for many law grads—it seems like everywhere we look, we see news of yet another law firm cutting back on its associate class, laying off lawyers, or closing its doors!

But while there may be fewer big firm opportunities in 2L summer work and 3L recruiting, there are still plenty of opportunities out there, says William Chamberlain, Assistant Dean and Clinical Assistant Professor of Law at the Center for Career Strategy & Advancement at Northwestern University School of Law. Like many other fields, legal work is cyclical, Chamberlain adds encouragingly: Hiring goes through ups and downs periodically and will increase again.

And while you can't change the economy, you can change your reaction to it, Chamberlain says.

The key to finding a job in tough times is to be flexible—don't be too specific about practice areas or work environments, and certainly don't expect to be hired by any one particular employer, says Chamberlain. Students must broaden their horizons; for example, Chamberlain believes that hiring will be on the upswing at smaller firms, which typically offer lower-cost options and may be sought out by corporate clients looking to cut costs. He also says that regulatory work may increase, creating some jobs for new grads as well. So, stay flexible and keep an open mind when looking for employment, Chamberlain says.

Chamberlain also says students must go back to basics when it comes to job searching. Students need to be more proactive than just trusting the on-campus interview process, Chamberlain says: They need to actively search for jobs, network with attorneys, and use the career services office at their school to assist with employment searches.

Finally, students must broaden their definition and understanding of networking. As I've said many times before, networking isn't about awkward small talk at cocktail parties; it's about making connections and building professional relationships. Take any chance to meet attorneys, Chamberlain says, whether through continuing legal education seminars, professional organizations, or social groups.

Originally published in The National Jurist, *January 2009 issue*

What If You Can't Find Employment?

It could happen to you...while you may have a stellar resume and skill set, you might not get that coveted first position right out of law school. The legal landscape – much like the economy itself – is cyclical:

If you're without a job, there are several practical tips you can implement to keep you moving in the right direction:

- First and foremost, maintain a positive attitude and be careful with how you present yourself. Employers won't hire you if you're constantly blogging about your job search–related complaints.

- Use your time wisely, says Gina Walcott, Executive Director of Lawyers Concerned for Lawyers, Inc., in Massachusetts. Think about all the people, places, and things you might have neglected or overlooked in recent years, and use this time to reconnect with people and to tackle some of those projects, Walcott advises, and you will feel a sense of accomplishment and a sense of connectedness.

  As an added benefit, you never know from where your next opportunity will come, Walcott adds: One of those people you reconnect with may prove useful in helping you to determine next steps, to come up with contacts that you might not have thought of, or may have some great ideas or avenues for you to pursue or incorporate in your job search.

- Work towards an improved and more marketable you, says Walcott. In particular, she recommends taking courses, learning new skills, honing and updating your current skill set, and evaluating what you want to do next.

- Keep up a routine, says Walcott, so you won't feel as if you are aimlessly wandering from day to day, but instead feel like you have purpose.

- Identify and write down your largest source(s) of stress, Walcott recommends.

- Eat healthier, exercise more, and laugh more, says Walcott.

- Shift your perspective—rather than looking at this as the worst thing that's ever happened to you, look at it as an incredible opportunity to reevaluate where you stand personally and professionally, says Walcott.

Summation

- Consider formal interviewing, online applications, and informal job searching and networking as part of your job search.

- Do your diligent research: Explore potential employers and understand the requirements and qualifications you'll need to have for each position that you apply for.

- Customize your applications and supporting materials according to the particular position.

- Don't discount yourself, keep an open mind, and be proactive about your job search.

- Remember to be polite, comport with professional etiquette, and stay positive during the job search.

Homework

- Sit down with a person who's knowledgeable about the legal landscape in your area, such as a career counselor, coach, or recruiter. Ask the person the following questions:

    - What fields, practice areas, legal environments, or particular employers are hiring in my location right now? (Or, if relocating interests you, ask about other locations where legal employers may be hiring.)

    - What fields, environments, or employers may be a good fit for my skill set?

    - What places or sources do you recommend to job seekers who are looking for an entry-level legal position?

    - What mistakes have you seen job seekers make in the past, and how can I avoid those mistakes?

    - What advice do you give new lawyers like me who are looking for a job?

- Make a list of places where you can start your job search. Include formal interviewing opportunities, online and print resources, and opportunities for informal job searching.

CHAPTER 4

TIPS FOR CRAFTING YOUR RESUME AND OTHER WRITTEN MATERIALS

This chapter offers tips for polishing your resume, cover letters, writing samples, job applications, and other written materials.

Resume Tips for Law Students and Recent Law Grads

First and foremost, law students and new lawyers need to recognize the ways that legal employers are different from employers in other fields. Remember that the legal profession is a fairly conservative one. What may be considered innovative in another field (such as sending a resume with elaborate graphics and pretty fonts to impress a creative employer) may land your resume at the bottom of the pile at a law firm. Your best bet is to stick with a conservative approach to resume writing. For example:

- As a rule of thumb, use the same font as the Courts would require—for the most part, this will mean sticking to Times New Roman or perhaps Courier.

- Don't use gimmicks. A resume sent via e-mail that plays music when the file is opened is not something that will make a positive impression on most legal employers.

- Phrase everything in a conservative way. Don't use abbreviations, slang, or informal language.

What should go into your resume in terms of content and substance? As a good rule of thumb, if you're fresh out of law school—less than five years of legal experience, as some career services experts put it—then you should limit your resume to a page unless you have important experience that you feel is essential to include in order to make the best impression possible, advises Mandie Araujo, Director of Career Services at New England Law|Boston. (Note: For candidates with more than five years of legal experience, a recommended two-page limit seems to be the general consensus.)

Remember that legal employers are extremely busy and may spend just seconds on each applicant's resume, Araujo points out. That said, list your most important attributes, skills, and accomplishments (your "best arguments," if you will) up front at the beginning of your resume, Araujo says. You want those arguments to be the ones that potential employers don't miss.

In terms of specific content and substance, Araujo explains that the following sections should be on your resume:

- First, list your contact information, including your name, address, phone number, and professional e-mail.

- Then, list your bar admissions and memberships. This section tells the employer in which jurisdictions you have been admitted to practice law.

- Next, list your education, including honors, awards, and activities. Begin with your Juris Doctor. Then, list any other graduate degrees, and finally, list your undergraduate degrees. You needn't include information about your high school education.

- Next, list your legal experience (paid employment in the legal field and any internships, clerkships, or other unpaid legal experience). Use bullet points to highlight the most important work you performed, states Araujo, and describe the work that you did with active verbs that signal responsibility and a strong work ethic.

  Use present-tense verbs for current employment and past-tense for past employment, and avoid the use of pronouns, Araujo adds.

- Following that, also list any other professional or work experience that may be of interest to potential legal employers, Araujo notes.

- You should also consider adding a separate section detailing the specialized skills you possess that are relevant to the position, as well as the languages you speak and your level of ability.

- Finally, Araujo recommends including a section that details your interests or hobbies outside of work—this, she says, can be a good interview conversation starter.

Once you've got the content and substance of your resume down, format your resume. Use a format that's easy to read, clean, and concise, Araujo advises. Stay consistent with your fonts and margins. If you're sending your resume through the mail, print it on high-quality resume paper. If you're sending it via e-mail, be sure the format that you intend to send is the same format that ultimately shows up in the recipient's inbox—Araujo recommends saving your resume in PDF format to avoid formatting mishaps.

Perhaps most importantly, make sure that your resume comports with the following three cardinal rules, which you MUST adhere to:

- Be sure that everything in your resume is truthful, accurate, relevant, and current, Araujo stresses.

- Put your best foot forward and make a great first impression.

- Remember that your resume is a marketing tool and should help you stand out as an individual, Araujo notes. Your resume may not be the one thing that ultimately gets you the job, but it may be the thing that gets you in the door!

THE ANSWERS—REVEALED!

Q: Should I re-draft my entire resume each time I submit it to a potential employer, and should I only submit it to firms that are in line with my interests?

A: First, a total rewrite is not necessary, says Kristin Oliveri, firm-wide Human Resources Manager at Baker Hostetler, LLP. If you're submitting to various different types of employers, you might customize your resume to better pinpoint your relevant qualifications and set you apart from others—for instance, have one resume for large firms and another for corporate law departments. But law firms typically like to see a wide range of experience and interests for summer and junior associate positions, so you won't necessarily take yourself out of the running if you list your Law Review article on the Sarbanes-Oxley Act and the firm happens to focus primarily on litigation. Listing your professional and personal interests, such as volunteer work and extracurricular activities, is generally a good idea, Oliveri advises.

As for submitting your resume only to certain types of employers or boutique law firms, Oliveri cautions students to keep an open mind. If you're only interested in a particular type of employer—for example, public interest firms— then it may serve you well not to send your resume to others, but limiting yourself to small firms in a sole practice area may make little sense as a law student or recent grad, Oliveri says. You might get into a law firm with pre-set expectations only to discover that the practice area you've had your heart set on since college isn't for you after all.

Originally published in The National Jurist, *September 2007 issue*

Writing a Great Cover Letter

A great cover letter can truly set you apart from other applicants. Cover letters serve many purposes:

- They introduce you to the prospective employer.

- They allow you to highlight your greatest strengths and skills.

- They allow you to note why your skill set is a good fit for the particular position.

- They allow you to tell a story—to show the employer one or two major accomplishments, as well as the ways in which they relate to the position.

- They can put a "human" touch on the sometimes mechanical approach applicants use to craft their resumes.

- They can serve as a writing sample, letting the potential employer glimpse into your professional writing style and ability. (Note this last purpose carefully—and consider it when you're drafting your cover letters, which should always be as professionally written as possible and proofread before they are sent out.)

A cover letter should typically be fairly short—perhaps four or five paragraphs long. At least one of those paragraphs should focus on your fit for the position. You shouldn't merely use the cover letter to restate your skills and qualifications; after all, that's what your resume is for! Rather, showcase the way that those skills and qualifications can best serve the employer and fit the particular position. Tie your accomplishment in with the employer's mission and goals for the position.

Consider the following examples:

- Don't just restate that you successfully defended an indigent client at your law student clinic; instead, show how the skills you gained during that representation can translate into success as an entry-level attorney working in criminal defense.

- Don't just restate that your appellate brief won an award in a writing competition; instead, show how a firm will benefit from your superior research and writing skills on the many motions, briefs, and memoranda that the job will require.

- Don't just restate that you drafted five important contracts during your summer associate position; instead, show how your drafting experience will help you work on contracts for corporate clients as a new associate at the firm.

Format your cover letter as a professional letter (think of the client letters you had to draft in law school and use the same format and approach). Even if you're sending the cover letter and resume via e-mail, use a business letter format, with a formal heading, greeting, body, and complimentary close. As with any other piece of writing that you'll send to a prospective employer, you should proofread your cover letter several times. Even better, ask a trusted source to read the letter for you and give you feedback on content, substance, and format.

Polishing Your Writing Sample

Many legal employers require a writing sample at some point in the application process, whether it's a required sample to be sent with your resume or a sample you're asked to provide at the interview.

Your writing sample serves many purposes: It allows a potential employer to gauge your analytical and writing skills, it provides a glimpse into the kind and quality of work product you may turn out at the job, it presents the employer with an idea of your professional writing style, and it allows you to showcase some of your knowledge on a legal issue or topic.

The following are some rules of thumb for writing samples:

- Provide a legal writing sample. Your college term paper on Victorian literature may have gotten you the highest grade in the class, but you're being judged on the basis of your legal writing ability, so provide a sample that allows the employer to gauge your professional legal writing style. Some examples may include

- A memorandum or section of a brief you drafted for your legal writing course

- A pleading or motion you drafted during an internship or summer associate position at a law firm

- A seminar paper on a legal topic that you wrote for a survey course in law school

- A client letter you drafted in your law school's clinic

- Be mindful of your tone and content. You may have written a great letter to the editor on the topic of immigration law, but that hot topic may be considered incendiary or be interpreted differently from your point of view by your interviewer.

  Stick with analytical writing that showcases your skills in applying the law to the facts or persuasive writing that requires you to argue on the basis of past precedent as it applies to a set of facts. Avoid political topics or topics that are likely to make for an argumentative read. And above all else, stay formal and professional in your writing—don't use slang, off-color humor, or informal language.

- Proofread and revise as necessary before you send out your sample. Check your spelling, grammar, organization, paragraph construction, and writing style. Better yet, ask a trusted source (such as a professor, a lawyer you know well, or a law school administrator) to read your sample and provide you with constructive feedback on it. Treat the writing sample as you would treat work product on the job: Provide outstanding writing that reflects your best work.

- If possible, check with the employer about its writing sample requirements. Some employers may have a very specific type of sample in mind when they ask you to provide one; check the employer's preferences when possible, whether in the job description or by consulting with the person in charge of recruiting.

- Bring a writing sample with you to the interview, even if you haven't been formally asked for it by the employer. Don't wait for them to ask you: Be proactive in providing outstanding work samples, just as you'd be proactive in other aspects of your job search.

Letters of Recommendation and References

Many employers also ask for several professional references or even letters of recommendation during the application process. While the employer is considering hiring you, other people's impressions of you as a professional can play an important part in determining whether you have the skill set needed for the job and whether you will be a good fit for the firm.

A letter of reference or recommendation for employment should serve as a tool to introduce you to the potential employer. A letter of reference should ideally be a glowing recommendation for you, yet it's important to note that all letters provided should be written honestly, expressing the letter writer's truthful impressions of you as a professional. Letters should include the following information:

- The letter writer's professional relationship to you and the capacity in which the letter writer knows you

- The length of time for which the letter writer has known you

- The letter writer's impressions of your skill set and your greatest strengths

- The letter writer's prediction as to whether you are a good fit for the particular position for which you are applying

- The letter writer's recommendation as to whether you should be hired for the position

Rather than ask you to provide letters, many employers will ask you for contact information for several references and then will follow up with the references on their own. When providing contact information for your references in writing to a potential employer, use a separate sheet of paper with the same heading as your resume, recommends Araujo. List complete contact information for your references (Araujo recommends listing at least three), as well as the person's professional relationship to you.

As with writing samples, be proactive about providing references—bring them with you to the interview if you haven't had to provide them with your resume or application, and don't just list a line like "references available upon request" on your resume.

Perhaps most importantly, be sure you ask your contacts to serve as references in advance, before you provide their names to a potential employer. Who should serve as a reference? Someone who knows your work; someone who understands your strengths and skills in a professional capacity.

Some good examples of references include a former supervisor, a professor whom you worked with on a case in your law school's student clinic, an attorney who oversaw you as an intern or a summer associate, or a judge you clerked for during a semester.

Filling Out a Job Application and Related Documents

As a final consideration, you should also know how to fill out a job application and what information may be asked of you when you apply for your first job (this can be somewhat of a daunting process, especially if this is your first position out of school). To help with this, use the following checklist:

- Know and have on hand the vital personal information an employer may ask you for, such as your Social Security number, driver's license or identification number, and contact information.

- Bring with you information about your past employment and education. Employers usually ask for this information, so be prepared to provide it—don't flounder around trying to guess your undergraduate GPA or the name of your supervisor from that summer job three years ago.

- Expect that, depending on the position, you may have to submit to various background checks. An increasing number of legal employers will verify your past employment history, education, and personal information. Some employers—recognizing that lawyers have a fiduciary duty over clients' money—also check new associate applicants' credit history. Depending on the position, you may encounter even more in-depth background checks.

In addition, have a basic understanding of the documents you'll need to fill out when you start work, such as the W-4 tax form, any state and local tax documents that may be applicable, and the I-9 employment eligibility verification form.

Summation

- Present your resume, cover letter, writing samples, job applications, and any other written materials to a prospective employer as marketing materials designed to make you stand out as an individual among many other candidates.

- Be sure that everything you put in writing to a prospective employer is truthful, accurate, relevant, and current.

- Look through sample law student and recent law grad resumes to ensure that your content, substance, and format comport with what a legal employer is looking for. Also consult with your law school's career services office or another career professional for assistance.

- Use the cover letter as a tool to introduce you to the prospective employer, as well as a chance to show the employer ways that your skills are relevant to the particular position, making you a great fit for the firm.

- Remember to put your best foot forward when it comes to any written materials. Make your "best arguments" up front, and be professional, thorough, and polished in all of the written materials that you're submitting to a prospective employer.

- Be proactive about providing writing samples, references, and other information that the employer may use in determining whether to hire you—have all information with you or on hand, and don't wait for the employer to ask you to provide it!

- Ask contacts to serve as references before you provide their contact information to a prospective employer. Choose people who know you professionally and are familiar with your skills, your strengths, and how well you would fit into the particular position for which you are applying.

- Expect that many legal employers will ask you for detailed information about your background (which you should be prepared to provide) and may conduct a detailed pre-employment screening as well.

Homework

- Study three sample law student or recent law grad resumes. (Need to obtain samples? Ask your law school's career services office for them or check out www.vault. com for law student resume samples.) On each resume you read, take notes on the following questions:

  - Was the format used on the resume easy to read and easy on your eyes?

  - Was the resume consistent throughout—both in terms of substance and descriptions and format?

  - Did the resume include all necessary sections and information?

  - Was anything included on the resume that you think should have been left off?

  - Did you get a good sense of the resume writer's strongest skills?

- Did the resume writer use paragraphs and bullets effectively?

- Did the writer phrase his or her descriptions well? Are there any words, sentences, or even entire paragraphs that you would change?

- What was the resume's strongest point or attribute?

- What was the resume's weakest point or attribute?

- Would you hire this person based on the resume? Why or why not?

- Draft up your own resume, using the tips provided in this chapter, and ask three people to critique it using the same questions above.

- Put together a writing sample that showcases your professional writing skills and analytical skills.

CHAPTER 5

Presenting Yourself to a Potential Employer

M uch goes into presenting yourself to a potential employer: making a good first impression when meeting the employer and presenting a polished and professional image, both online and in real life. This chapter offers tips for polishing your self-presentation.

Meeting a Potential Employer

It's probably one of the most nerve-racking things you'll ever have to do. Meeting a potential employer for the first time can be daunting—after all, it's your first chance to make a great impression and your only chance to make a great first impression! Whether it's a formal interview or an informal networking opportunity, that first meeting is important.

Before meeting a potential employer for the first time, consider the following checklist:

- Check with the employer ahead of time about who at the firm you'll be meeting with. Then, find out some professional information about the person(s) that you can use to your advantage in conversation during the meeting: for example, where the person went to law school or what types of cases the person handles.

- Also check with the employer about the environment in which you'll be meeting—are you going to an office, having lunch at a restaurant, or meeting on campus at your law school, for example? Be familiar with the plans for the meeting so that you can have some level of comfort with the place and environment in which you'll be meeting with the potential employer.

- Be punctual. Avoid anything that could make you late. Get directions ahead of time and figure out what route you'll take to the meeting; arrange for ample time to tend to your obligations before you have to leave for the meeting; and leave early enough to account for potential traffic jams, late trains, and other potential calamities.

- Err on the side of being conservative and formal in your dress.

- No matter how relaxed you may be at the meeting or how friendly the potential employer may be, be sure to stay professional and courteous. Even when you feel that the meeting is going extremely well, don't get so relaxed that you let up on the level of formality and professionalism that's required, generally, in the workplace. Remember that you're trying to make a first impression as a professional—act like one!

- Show enthusiasm about the potential employer. Prepare some pointed questions about the position, the firm, or the employer ahead of time so that you can ask them during the meeting.

- Have your "career sound bites" at the ready (see the "Crafting Your 'Career Sound Bites'" section later in this chapter) so that you can readily share information about your career and your accomplishments when the employer asks you to do so.

- Bring with you extra copies of anything that the potential employer may ask for. This includes business cards or other contact information, your resume, your references, and even a writing sample.

- If you happen to meet a potential employer in an unplanned, happenstance kind of way, don't panic and stay confident! Put on a warm smile, convey your interest and enthusiasm, and strike up a conversation that will allow you to put your best foot forward and make a great first impression.

Presenting Yourself to a Potential Employer: Polishing Your Professional Image

Presenting a professional image, to me, has three distinct components: It means exuding professionalism in person, in writing, and online. Several adjectives make up a young professional, in my opinion, including

- Confident

- Able

- Approachable

- Mature

- Courteous

- Polite

- Diligent

- Timely

Appearance matters, believes Janet Hutchinson, Assistant Dean for Career Services at Emory University School of Law, and a professional and polished image can go a long way. Recognize that many supervising attorneys, older attorneys, and others in the firm may not be receptive to you being casual in the office—err on the side of being formal.

Also recognize the value of "face time," says Hutchinson: Amidst the e-mails and IMs, make time to present yourself in person as a young professional. Also work hard to ensure that your professional reputation stays intact, Hutchinson points out: For example, keep your commitments, treat your peers well, and don't burn any bridges.

An employer's professional image of you is crafted from multiple pieces of information, says Dean David Logan of Roger Williams University School of Law. A good first impression is hard to lose, and a bad first impression can be hard to overcome, Dean Logan says. Projecting confidence and self-assuredness is a part of presenting yourself as a professional— but this is not an argument for (unearned) cockiness or swagger, Dean Logan explains. Rather, he explains it as a preference for

- A firm handshake

- A steady gaze

- A friendly and approachable manner

This is going to give your superiors an early sense that you are presentable to clients and that you will be able to navigate the turbulent and uncertain waters that all lawyers now face, Dean Logan explains.

THE ANSWERS—REVEALED!

Q: What do you think about using nontraditional and innovative methods to capture a potential employer's attention?

A: It depends on how innovative we're talking. I recently read an article on a general job search Web site about "innovative" ways job seekers are seeking to stand out—including blogging, using music and graphics in their resumes, and even wearing a "hire me" shirt to the interview. But are these methods ever acceptable in the legal field?

Probably not—in many ways, the legal field is a pretty conservative profession, explains Beverly Bracker, Director of Career Services at Thomas Jefferson School of Law. Persistence, creativity, and persuasion can capture a potential employer's attention, but you should aim to project those qualities through professional networking.

Blogging may be one "innovative" way to make you stand out among others—but only if you do it right. Skip personal blogs and write about professional issues instead, Bracker says, like developments in a practice area that interests you or your experiences helping out with a student organization or studying the law abroad. Don't use names, and remember to stay professional, respectful, and positive in your blog posts, Bracker adds.

Originally published in The National Jurist, *February 2009 issue.*

Crafting Your "Career Sound Bites"

Imagine that you're networking or interviewing for a job and you come across the following questions from a colleague, an interviewer, or a potential contact.

What will you say in response?

Don't get caught by surprise: Prepare an answer that makes you sound good. Construct a 30-second "sound bite" to relay your answers concisely, clearly, and comprehensively.

Q: What do you do?

_____

_____

_____

Q: What would you like to do during your first year as a lawyer?

_____

_____

_____

Q: What do you bring to the table?

_____

_____

_____

Q: Why should we hire you?

_____

_____

_____

Presenting a Professional Image Online and Over E-mail

It's no secret that many employers are increasingly relying on the Internet to find and vet applicants. Many employers are looking up potential candidates online to find out information about them.

For example, an employer may search for a potential candidate using Google to find out about the candidate's professional accomplishments, as well as to find out enough about the candidate personally to help the employer determine whether the candidate is a good fit for the firm. As a result, your online image—the image and messages you put forth on your Web sites; on social networking sites such as Facebook, MySpace, and LinkedIn; on blogs; on message boards and discussion groups; and over e-mail—must be just as professional as your image "in real life."

Here are some examples of online conduct that may turn off a potential employer:

- Conduct that signals that you may be untrustworthy or unable to maintain confidentiality. If you maintain a blog on which you are constantly gossiping about others, your conduct may make a potential employer think twice about trusting you with client matters.

  Remember the importance of maintaining confidentiality, and don't post anything online that may signal to a potential employer that you won't be able to keep things confidential.

- Conduct that signals that you may have some serious issues with stress, alcohol or substance abuse, gambling, and other potential personal problems. Some stress is normal—legal employers likely remember what it's like to be stressed as a law student and recent law graduate, so a stressed-out post about your upcoming Commercial Law final isn't likely to jeopardize your chances of employment. Constant stress and complaining, on the other hand, might—as might any indication that you deal with that stress in an unhealthy manner, such as by abusing alcohol or other substances.

  As a rule of thumb, never allow anything about you to appear on the Internet that you wouldn't want to be seen by your employer or your mother, offers Dean David Logan of Roger Williams University School of Law. In particular, use extreme care on social networking sites because other people can post digital material that includes you, Dean Logan points out, and the other poster may not have the same need to display professionalism (or even have an accurate sense of what professionalism is).

- Conduct that signals previous or current issues with criminal or unethical conduct. In college, it may have seemed like a good idea to film your friends pulling off a prank through illegal conduct, but a potential employer won't look lightly on a video that shows your involvement or participation in illegal activity. Remember that ethics rules prohibit attorneys from engaging in criminal conduct, and act accordingly both in real life and online.

- Conduct that signals that you may not be a good fit at the firm. For example, you may be broadcasting overly zealous political beliefs that may not mesh with the mission of the firm or the messages the firm is trying to send, or you may be turning off a specific kind of employer by blatantly blogging about not wanting to work in a particular firm environment or practice area. Be aware of the implications of posting any personal beliefs that could turn off a potential employer.

- Conduct that signals that you may not be serious about joining the firm. If you're telling a potential employer in Boston that you're interested in accepting a position and yet freely blogging or posting online about wanting to relocate to the Midwest, you can expect that the Boston employer will think twice about offering you the job. Likewise, if you're freely posting about wanting to join one particular firm at which you've interviewed, you might turn off other firms who might have wanted to extend you an offer.

- Conduct that signals improperly relaxed or informal relationships with peers and colleagues. E-mail is considered by many to be a more informal means of communication, but don't let that fool you: Any communication with a potential employer, colleague, and even professional peers should be formal and professional, even e-mails, instant messages, and the like.

Be very careful with e-mail, recommends Dean Logan: for example, he points out that "delete" doesn't completely delete; that hitting "reply all" rather than "reply" can be disastrous; and that typos are an even bigger risk with tiny iPhone or BlackBerry keyboards and screens, especially when the message is sent on the go.

Less appreciated is the fact that e-mail can come across as curt, says Dean Logan, adding that he recommends the formality of old-fashioned forms of correspondence — even with any perceived hassle associated with them! Unless the junior lawyer knows the recipient's preferences, e-mail can seem excessively informal, Dean Logan says, and the slower pace of "snail mail" also reduces the risk of firing off an intemperate reply.

- Conduct that signals that you don't take your professional obligations or career plans completely seriously. Your law school buddies may have gotten a kick out of your juvenile screen name or e-mail address, but a potential employer won't. Remember that legal employers are pretty conservative, and use screen names and e-mail addresses that are conservative, formal, and professional as well. You usually can't go wrong with some variation of your first and last name.

THE ANSWERS—REVEALED!

Q: How can I ensure that I'm projecting a professional image online, and why is it important to do so?

A: Students are often shocked to find out that employers are looking through online profiles and conduct when hiring, says Paula Nailon, Assistant Dean for Professional

Development at the University of Arizona Rogers College of Law. From social networking sites to blogs to personal and family Web sites, legal employers are increasingly checking up on a candidate's online image. In fact, Nailon adds that some bar associations also check all information available to them when conducting a character and fitness exam for admission—and that information may include online sources.

That can mean trouble if you have posted information that's incriminating or unprofessional. For example, Nailon says that really strong political views may turn off an employer: The reason employers run online searches is not only to find information that a background check won't uncover, but also to help gauge the applicant's fit with the firm. More subtle content—like blogging about stress, alcohol or substance abuse, gambling, and other issues—can also be a turn-off, Nailon adds, so think twice before you post. Remember that online content is permanent—something you delete can still be cached and later pulled up, Nailon warns. Even a screen name or e-mail address can make you look unprofessional to a potential employer or a professor whom you're asking for a recommendation.

Still, there are some great ways to use the Internet to your advantage when trying to build your professional reputation. For instance, you can publish articles about your interest in a particular practice area to help get your name out there in a positive light, Nailon says. Likewise, you can blog about a presentation you gave, volunteer work you did, or a student organization you created.

Originally published in The National Jurist, *January 2009 issue*

Summation

- When meeting a potential employer for the first time, be as prepared for the meeting as possible: Know in advance the environment in which you'll meet the employer, know who specifically you'll be meeting with, prepare questions for the employer in advance, and be prepared to share information about your career that will present you in the best possible light.

- Remember to be confident, formal, and professional when meeting any potential employer for the first time.

- Err on the side of being conservative and formal in your dress and demeanor.

- Present yourself as a professional in person, in writing, and online.

- Avoid conduct (both online and in "real life") that may paint you as untrustworthy, unethical, or unprofessional.

Homework

- Craft your career sound bites. Then, think of any additional questions that you've been asked before by a potential employer, a supervisor, or a professor. Craft career sound bites for those additional questions as well.

- Make a list of ten things that you consider the most important in presenting a professional image. Keep the list with you. Periodically (once a week or so) check your list and make sure that you are sticking to it—that your conduct hasn't veered from the "professional conduct rules" you had set for yourself.

CHAPTER 6

Interviewing Tips

This chapter offers advice for successfully navigating the interviewing process, including on-campus interviews, call-back interviews, small-firm interviews, and more.

What Does the On-Campus Interview Process Entail?

Typically, large law firms and some government and business employers use on-campus interviewing (OCI) to conduct initial interviews with potential candidates. Many firms interview second-year law students for summer positions, while firms and other employers also use OCI to begin the interviewing process for long-term employment prospects.

Many firms have very formal OCI schedules: They post in advance at which campuses they will interview and on what dates. Your school's OCI process will most likely be coordinated by the school's career services office, and you will have to sign up in advance for interview slots.

OCIs are quick: You can expect to spend perhaps twenty to thirty minutes on each interview. Based on your interview and general qualifications, you may then be called back for a second interview, which typically takes place at the firm or employer and entails interviewing with several people who are in charge of hiring.

What Questions Can You Expect During OCI?

Because this is generally the first time you'll meet an interviewer, your resume is pretty much the only information on which the interviewer can base his or her questions. Therefore, you should always be prepared to discuss anything on your resume, says Susan Galli, Hiring Partner and Chair of the Hiring Committee at Ropes & Gray, LLP. Galli adds that she does not use a template list of questions, but rather formulates questions based on the individual.

Many interviewers will ask candidates to explain specific parts of their resumes in more detail. For example:

- What challenges have you encountered during an externship?

- What did you accomplish at a summer position?

- What was the most rewarding part of serving on law review?

- What was the hardest part of law school for you?

- What interested you in going to law school?

- What did you learn during the mock trial competitions you attended?

- What would you describe as the most beneficial part of your law school experience?

In addition, you can also expect questions about fit. Interviewers are trying to ascertain that you are familiar with the firm and will be a good fit for the firm—and vice versa—so you can expect questions like these:

- What attracts you to our firm?

- Are you familiar with the practice areas in which our firm practices?

- Are you familiar with the attorneys who work at our firm?

- What have you recently found out about our firm that surprised you?

- What differentiates our firm from other firms in your mind?

What Are Some Questions that You Should Be Asking During Interviews?

A successful initial interview should not be an interrogation, but rather a conversation that flows naturally between the interviewer and the candidate, says John Siamas, a partner in charge of recruiting at Reed Smith, LLP, and Dean of Litigation at the firm's Reed Smith University. Galli adds that she is always happy to discuss anything the candidate wants to talk about.

Definitely do your research before the interview, recommends Coke Cherney, partner at Ropes & Gray and a member of the firm's hiring committee. At minimum, you should be familiar with the firm and its work through information on the firm's Web site. Most recruiters have encountered candidates who came to the interview unprepared, and it shows. You don't want to be the candidate who appears unenthusiastic—or worse, asks, "Remind me what firm this is again?"

Still, recruiters agree that it is best not to sound rehearsed when asking questions about the firm—canned questions won't get you a lot of points with interviewers, says Cherney. Instead of asking the questions that you think you are supposed to ask (like questions about the firm's training or pro bono programs, which is something that nearly every candidate asks about), Cherney says it's essential to inquire about the things that are important to you personally.

Siamas agrees that personal tastes and interests should come across at the initial interview. He adds that he always asks candidates what their passions are—and if they answer by giving a practice area, Siamas says he follows up with a "Really?" to encourage conversation about the person's interests. Again, interviewers look for individual answers rather than rehearsed statements, and they are more likely to remember and call back a candidate who stands out for a unique passion or interest.

Remember also that the interview should be a conversation—not just a one-way speech! You should aim to ask the potential employer some questions about the firm, and come prepared with some pointed, specific questions and queries. (As some career counselors will tell you, if the employer asks you whether you have any questions, and you answer "no," you may as well write off your chances of being called back for a follow-up interview!)

Some examples of questions you may choose to ask include the following:

- What, in your opinion, differentiates your firm from others?

- What skills and character traits do you look for in entering associates?

- What is one particular case or project that you've worked on that you are particularly proud of?

- What is the most important information you tell your potential clients about your firm or your practice?

In addition to the importance of asking general questions such as the ones listed above, it's essential that you do your research and come prepared with some specific and pointed questions for your interviewers. For example:

- Check the firm's Web site for bios of the people who are going to interview you. Ask specific follow-up questions about the interviewers' background, practice, and professional experience. For instance, if you see that the person works in a niche practice area, ask him or her what the most challenging or most rewarding part of working in that field is.

- Check the firm's Web site for news and press releases about the firm's recent cases, activities, and projects, and then ask about them. For example, if you see that the firm recently had a victory in an important case or a significant settlement, offer a positive comment on that case and ask a follow-up question.

- Check the firm's brochure for interesting tidbits of information. Say, for example, that the firm is the first firm in your region to experiment with a particular practice or has had a significant amount of business in a particular area—again, offer a positive comment and then ask a follow-up question. As with any other part of the interview, the key to asking questions is to show genuine interest, enthusiasm, and a positive attitude about interviewing with the firm.

What Are Interviewers Looking For in Candidates?

The interviewer is trying to ascertain the candidate's level of interest and enthusiasm for the law, legal practice, and the firm, says Siamas, adding that he looks for personal traits such as

- Good judgment

- Common sense

- Hard work

- A sense of ethics and responsibility

And what if nerves get the best of you and you give a less-than-stellar interview? Don't fret that your chances of being called back are gone. Most interviewers understand the pressures of the OCI process. Cherney says he gives students the benefit of the doubt, particularly during the first interview. But try to be relaxed and show engagement, enthusiasm, and confidence. Cherney says those traits can help you give a more pleasant interview and stand out among other candidates.

Some of the information about OCI in this section was originally published in my "Career Hotline" column in *The National Jurist*.

What Can You Expect During the Call-Back Interview?

While OCI happens on campus, call-back interviews generally take place on the firm's premises. Call-back interviews may be more detailed: Remember that an on-campus interview is formally structured and that many students interview with the firm in just one day, leaving no more than mere minutes for each interviewee to talk to the potential employer. Whereas OCI is just the first part of the process (and a way for the firm to separate candidates who aren't potential hires from those who may be), call-back interviews allow the employer to get to know potential hires better.

So, during a call-back interview, you'll likely meet with several members of the firm and interview with each. (You may find that you'll meet with attorneys, including partners and associates, and even support staff or human resources personnel at various levels.) In addition to finding out about your skills, abilities, and background, each of those interviewers is also looking at how you may fit into the firm: Are you the right person for the job, and are you a good fit for the firm's culture, environment, and organization?

You'll also likely be given a tour of the firm or at least be shown around. While you're walking around, be engaged and keep your eyes open. Observe the organization's culture and get a feel for what it's like to work at the firm.

If you're meeting with several interviewers, you should try to talk to the recruiter or interview coordinator and find out the names of the people you'll be interviewing with, recommends Mandie Araujo, Director of Career Services at New England Law|Boston. Consult the bios of all of them, have a good idea as to their backgrounds, and prepare pointed questions for each potential interviewer. Take care not to ask the same questions of everyone you meet, Araujo notes. Instead, prepare a customized set of questions for each person, which will help you show that you're prepared, interested, and engaged during the interview process.

Note that you may also be asked to meet with more than one person at the same time during call-back interviews — it may be worth it to practice interviewing in a setting that forces you to talk to multiple people at once so that you're not taken aback when you have to do the same thing on a real interview.

Finally, note that you may also be asked to conduct the interview over coffee or a meal or to conduct it in a social setting of some sort; again, it's best that you prepare for that possibility by practicing how to act and behave in a similar setting, Araujo says. For instance, attend a bar association event or function and get a feel for what it's like to talk with other professionals in a social setting.

Whatever happens during the interview (and wherever you may be taken for that meal), be sure you don't get too relaxed, Araujo says. Remember that you're being evaluated not just on what you say but also on how you act, what type of professional image you project, and how well you'll fit into the firm's organizational culture.

If you're going to the firm's premises, remember that the interview begins the moment that you set foot inside the firm! From the first moment that you arrive, remember to stay professional and courteous to everyone you meet. Being rude to a receptionist or support staff is one potential way to make a bad first impression on the employer who finds out about your impolite conduct later.

What Can You Expect at an Interview with a Smaller Firm or Other Employer?

Much of what you can expect when interviewing with smaller firms really depends on the firm and the attorneys interviewing you. Where large law firms may have a more structured and formal approach as to what takes place during the interviewing process (for example, starting with OCI, then offering call-back interviews only at specific time intervals), smaller firms will interview in the way that makes the most sense for the firm, its culture, and its environment. At one firm, you may find that you'll have one full day of interviews with several people; at another, you may find that you land the job through networking and the interview is not much more than a mere formality.

Whatever approach the firm employs when interviewing potential candidates, you must make sure that you are preparing for each interview as thoroughly and appropriately as you would be when taking part in a large firm's formal interview process. This means you must research the employer ahead of time, come prepared to share pertinent information and ask questions about yourself as a potential hire, come prepared to ask pointed questions about the employer and to follow up on questions that you may be asked during the interview, and always aim to present a professional image.

How Can You Project a Professional Image During the Interview?

Appearing professional, competent, and confident is essential to nailing the interview. Potential employers judge you not only on what you say and present during the interview, but also how you present it. Here are some pointers to get you started:

- Be prepared. Do your research; bring copies of anything that you may be asked for; prepare pointed and relevant questions to ask about the firm; and make sure that you account and prepare for any potential glitches that may come up before or during the interview.

- Project confidence and competence. Remember that the interview is your chance to show the employer why you are the right person for the job.

- On the other hand, don't just focus on yourself—focus on how your skills and your abilities fit in with what the employer is looking for. Understand what the job entails, and each time you answer a question, show the potential employer the ways in which you could further the mission and business of the firm.

- Show interest. Stay engaged throughout the interview, and show that you genuinely want to work for the employer.

- Dress the part. You can't go wrong with a formal business suit in most cases, but if possible, check with the employer about its own dress code to ensure that you are comporting with it during the interview.

- Act the part. Follow the rules of common courtesy; be polite and approachable; and no matter how well the interview is going, don't get too informal!

- Go into the interview with the right attitude and mindset. Project energy, enthusiasm, and positivity in your demeanor.

- Follow up. This is the cardinal rule of interviewing—yet many new lawyers fail to adhere to it. Send a thank-you card to every person who interviewed you, and share some specific information about the interview (such as something new you learned about the firm or something that intrigued or interested you) as part of your note to show that you are engaged and genuinely interested in the firm.

Summation

- Familiarize yourself with the interview process used by different firms and employers, whether you're participating in the formal OCI process or interviewing with smaller firms or other employers.

- Be prepared for the kinds of questions you may be asked, and be ready to share information about yourself in a confident and constructive manner.

- Remember that you need to show the employer why you are the right person for the job—focus on why you are a good fit for the firm (and vice versa) and how you can help promote the firm's mission, practice, and business.

- Do your research about the employer before you come to the interview. Come up with pointed questions to ask about the firm.

- Prepare for the unexpected!

- Always project a professional image, show genuine enthusiasm and interest in the firm, and maintain a positive attitude.

- Follow up!

Homework

- Ask a trusted friend or colleague (or better yet, a trusted supervisor, administrator, or professor) to conduct a mock interview with you. Have the person ask you the questions earlier in this chapter, and then practice asking the person some of the questions you should be asking a potential employer.

- Write down ten traits that make for an interesting interview subject. Which of those traits do you possess? Which ones do you still need to hone?

- Practice being on the other side of the interview: Conduct informational interviews with attorneys and others. Note (to yourself!) what you liked and disliked about the interviewee's answers and image. Remember: the more you practice interviewing, the more polished, professional, and confident you'll appear during actual job interviews.

PART II

MAKING THE MOST OF YOUR FIRST YEAR

Chapter 7: Learning on the Job

Chapter 8: Getting Meaningful Assignments

Chapter 9: Increasing Your Marketability and Building Your Client Base

Chapter 10: Increasing Your Productivity—and Your Billing

Chapter 11: Building Your Network

Chapter 12: Organizing Your Work and Your Life, Managing Your Time, and Managing Your Money

Chapter 13: Ethics, Professionalism, Workplace Etiquette, and Interacting with Others

Chapter 14: Maintaining Work-Life Balance, Preventing Burnout, and Managing Your Stress Level

CHAPTER 7

LEARNING ON THE JOB

The first year of your career should be all about learning on the job. This chapter offers you tips, resources, and advice.

What Makes the First Year Potentially the Most Difficult?

As many people will tell you, the first year of doing anything new is often the most difficult—transitions, whether they deal with your career or life events, can be difficult, and they often come with a steep learning curve.

But just what, specifically, makes the first year on the job as a new lawyer difficult? Here are some of the experts' takes:

- Making the switch from law school, where students have a lot of flexibility, to billing many hours at an intense position comes with difficulty, says William Chamberlain, Assistant Dean of the Center for Career Strategy & Advancement at Northwestern University School of Law. For some students—particularly those who have never had a job—being the lowest person on the totem pole is also difficult: You're transitioning from your role as graduating student into a new role as a brand-new associate.

- Some students may be surprised at how hard they'll have to work as lawyers, says Dean Richard Matasar of New York Law School. They may underestimate the (very heady) difficulty of taking responsibility for clients' legal issues—and the realization that a lawyer's mistakes can affect the lives of many other people.

- Part of the difficulty is that the classroom isn't all that great at preparing students for the practice of law, adds Beverly Bracker, Director of Career Services at Thomas Jefferson School of Law. Also, some new lawyers may get frustrated by the lack of feedback on the job.

- Much of the law school curriculum is theoretical, says Janet Hutchinson, Assistant Dean for Career Services at Emory University School of Law. All those courses you had to take as a law student may have taught you the basics about the law, but they probably haven't taught you how things play out in practice. Couple that with the fact that most students get zero practical or clinical experience, and it makes for a difficult transition.

- In addition, not only are new lawyers going through a tough transition at work, but starting out as a lawyer is also a complete change in the way your life is structured, says Paula Zimmer, Assistant Dean and Director of Career Services at Western New England School of Law. Going from student to employee means you have to learn a brand-new way of living. Plus, time management can be a huge challenge as a new lawyer—not only on the job, but also outside the workplace.

- Plus, the transition from school to practice can be difficult for many graduates who do not understand that the practice of law is a business, says Trisha Fillbach, Director of Career Development at Drake Law School. While in law school, you review case law and statutes and dissect the thoughts and opinions of judges. You may even participate on a moot court team or on law review.

While all of this is great experience, students do not always remember that when it comes down to it, the practice of law is a business in which their time will be a commodity. They do not always know how to market themselves, sign the potential client, bill the client, get paid by the client, and—within this time frame—form a relationship with the client that will bring future business and referrals.

- To add to the mix, law students often go to law school right out of college with little or no work experience, points out Lisa Terrizzi, career coach and consultant and chairperson of the Massachusetts Bar Association's Lawyers in Transition Committee. As such, not only are new lawyers new to the practice of law—they are often new to the work world entirely, and they may not know how to handle difficult work situations that may arise every day.

- Part of that difficulty in getting accustomed to the workplace lies in learning to master the environment and the culture of your own firm, believes Mandie Araujo, Director of Career Services at New England Law|Boston. Law practice is very different from the law school environment, and recent grads who've never worked at a firm can find it challenging to adapt to their new surroundings.

Plus, while law school may prepare you to do lots of work in very little time, it doesn't always prepare you to work as smart as you should. As Araujo says, it can be difficult for new lawyers to grasp that time is of the essence and that their biggest selling point is their time, as well as to deliver under the constant time constraints and pressures of law practice.

What Does "Training" Really Mean When You're a New Lawyer?

Now that you've read about the most challenging parts of the job, it's important to note that all of the preceding areas can be learned—even mastered—during the first year. The key? Learn you must!

Although many law firms provide formal training and opportunities for professional development, you shouldn't just rely on your firm for learning, explains Dana Levin, U.S. Director of Legal Recruiting at Reed Smith, LLP. You should expect to be responsible for your own career and development, says Levin: Show that you enjoy having ownership and responsibility over your own work and look for opportunities to better yourself on the job.

Young lawyers must be willing to learn as much as possible, even if they think what they're learning has nothing to do with what they want to do in the future, says Rachel Littman, Assistant Dean for Career Development at Pace Law School. For starters, it's not uncommon for new lawyers to "fall into" a practice area or particular specialty—and you likely won't know exactly what you want to do until you've discovered and learned about many different things on the job. Plus, having an open mind and being amenable to learning signals to employers that you have a positive attitude on the job.

The best way to learn something new? Ask lots of questions—
both questions about specific tasks and questions about the
"big picture." For example, when you're assigned a new project or a task on a new case, ask questions about how that
project relates to your supervisor's overall strategy, the entire
transaction, or the firm's handling of the whole case, Littman
recommends.

Learning isn't limited to practical skills. You must also con-
sciously become an informed observer when it comes to your
work environment, says Terrizzi, by reading up on law practice in general and your areas of practice in particular as well
as by observing and learning about the organizational culture
and structure in place at your firm. You have to focus not only
on learning your technical areas, but also on appreciating the
critical need to master interpersonal skills.

After you've completed a task, follow up! Ask about how your
work fit into the overall picture, as well as what happened to
the case or transaction at the end. For example, if you were
asked to draft a motion in a case, you should not only follow
up on the end result on the motion, but also periodically check
in on how the case is going—and don't be afraid to ask if there
are any additional tasks that you could help out with. Many
new lawyers won't get to work on cases or transactions from
beginning to end, and supervisors may not think to explain
how each task helps the overall big picture, says Littman.
Plus, when you follow up on your own, you show interest and
pride in your work.

And what if you make a mistake? Own up to it as quickly
as possible, says Littman—and don't even think about lying,
cheating, or otherwise attempting to cover up your error. Most
employers understand that new lawyers are, after all, new to
the practice and will make mistakes as they learn; they won't,

however, take kindly to unethical or unprofessional behavior in covering up your mistakes.

After you've come clean, ask your employer what you can do to help fix the mistake and then be available and willing to help as needed. If things didn't go as well as you hoped on a particular task or project, go back and fix it to the extent possible, points out Janet Hutchinson, Assistant Dean for Career Services at Emory University School of Law, and aim to prove yourself the next time you are assigned the same or a similar task.

All in all, you should aim to learn enough during the first year to have a clear idea of what law practice is like, what day-to-day practice is like, and some things that you would like to continue learning about, says Hutchinson.

THE ANSWERS—REVEALED!

Q: Why is "informal training" important, and how can I make sure I will receive it on the job?

A: While law firms may impress candidates with their formal training programs, a firm's stance on informal training is just as important to its associates' professional development. Informal training can take on many forms: mentoring, career counseling, professional development evaluations, and informal events between associates and partners that focus on associates' development at the firm.

Informal training has always been significant to the process of becoming a skilled attorney, and apprenticeships have played an important part in legal training since the onset of the profession. Mentoring is natural, says Chris Aidun, partner and co-chair of Weil Gotschal's professional development committee, and mentors can help establish rapport, provide counseling and moral support, and answer career questions that associates may be reluctant to ask elsewhere. To encourage informal training, Weil Gotschal assigns mentors to all first-year associates, holds mentor-mentee luncheons, and has class monitor partners who oversee associate groups.

Much informal training involves feedback from experienced attorneys about associates' development and career track. At Hogan & Hartson, LLP, for example, associates prepare a yearly professional development plan, outlining their goals in terms of legal skills, substantive knowledge, client relations, and even the professional identity they'd like to create. They are assigned a mentor who helps them draft the plan and assists with implementing its goals throughout the year.

Informal training should be an integral factor in your job search, but this isn't the kind of information you'll necessarily read in the firm's brochure. To find out how important informal training is to your potential employers, your best bet is to talk with the firms' summer and junior associates: Like you, they value the mentoring they receive and can tell you about both formal and informal opportunities.

As for getting the most out of informal training, the key is active participation. A firm could offer all the training programs in the world, but they won't do any good if new associates don't take advantage of them, says Matt Bloch, partner at Weil Gotschal & Manges, LLP, who spearheaded the firm's professional development committee. If you don't participate in training opportunities, you are wasting your time, Aidun agrees—and risk being seen as a merely passive participant in your own career.

(continued)

(continued)

> Weil Gotschal has a "Jump Start" program where associates take required substantive courses in corporate law or litigation and graduate to a trial skills workshop weekend. The firm also put together a list of Associate Development Goals, which offer new associates guidance on the objectives they are expected to achieve at different levels of their careers. At Finnegan Henderson Farabow Garrett & Dunner, LLP, associates can participate in week-long trial advocacy courses and a deposition training course offered on-site by the National Institute of Trial Advocacy; the firm also employs a legal writer-in-residence who runs writing courses and offers one-on-one writing help.
>
> Some large law firms require all new associates to attend formal training programs. First-years at Cooley Godward Kronish, LLP, attend "Cooley College," where they receive practice tips through substantive lectures and skills development programs. And training doesn't stop with practice area seminars: Ropes & Gray, LLP, for instance, runs sessions on time management and negotiation skills for junior associates and management skills for senior associates.
>
> *Originally published in* The National Jurist, *October 2007 issue*

What Are Some Opportunities for Professional Development?

Professional development entails many things. Here are just some examples:

- Continuing substantive legal education, where you learn about a practice area or substantive area that interests you or is relevant to your job—for example, when taking a course on commercial leasing

- Skill-based and practical education, where you learn to hone a specific skill or skill set relevant to your work—for example, when attending a seminar on formulating deposition questions

- Business skills development, where you learn to hone the skills that will help you build your book of business and cultivate relationships with new and existing clients—for example, when attending a seminar on legal marketing techniques

- Technical skills development, where you learn to hone the technical skills that will help you on the job—for example, when attending a training class by an e-discovery provider about e-discovery best practices

- Social skills development, where you learn to hone the skills and techniques that are necessary for cultivating professional relationships—for example, when attending a networking reception

- Ethics education, where you learn about the rules of ethics and professional responsibility that govern attorneys' conduct—for example, when attending a lecture on the duty of confidentiality

- Career development, where you learn to make educated decisions about your career, such as self-assessment, career goals, and career next steps—for example, when attending a conference on alternative legal career options

Opportunities for professional development are all around you, and you should learn to take advantage of them as early on as possible in your career. Professional development helps you by honing specific skills that you'll need on the job, learning about a substantive area in more depth and detail, and even offering you chances to build your professional network while attending seminars and events.

Some large firms, government employers, and other large employers offer professional development programs in-house for their new lawyers and employees. For example, some larger firms have periodic formal on-the-job seminars and training (like Reed Smith, LLP's Reed Smith University), where new associates learn practical skills.

While some firms may employ a full-time professional development director to run and oversee training programs, others may periodically hire outside providers to come in and offer in-house training. Some firms even offer writing tips and writing instruction to their new associates. Some employers also run formal mentoring programs (see a detailed discussion of them later in this chapter).

But not every new lawyer is lucky enough to find professional development programs just down the hall—in most cases, particularly if you're working for a smaller firm, you'll have to seek out those opportunities on your own. (Still, you should note that many employers will reimburse you for the costs of attending pre-approved training programs.) Need some ideas about where you could find opportunities for professional development? Consider the following avenues:

- Your state's continuing legal education association

- A state, local, or national bar association

- A specialty bar association that focuses on a specific practice area

- A specialty bar association that focuses on serving a specific group, such as women or minorities

- The Young Lawyers section of a state, local, or national bar association

- Other trade associations for legal professionals, such as those representing law office management professionals

- A local law school

- Online providers

REVEALED!

"I read several magazines geared towards my area of practice, meet regularly with other practitioners, and participate in a local bar association that has many other practitioners in the same field.... Meeting other practitioners and keeping in contact is important to me since there are usually new or unusual aspects to my practice that I have not experienced previously. My professional contacts have been great in giving advice or helping me locate resources to answer my questions."

Christie Edwards, asylum attorney and adjunct professor; 2007 Thomas Jefferson School of Law graduate

How Can You Find Great Mentors?

First, it's important to note that while you'd be fortunate to have just one great mentor, you shouldn't limit yourself when it comes to mentoring relationships—the more mentors you find who can give you sound advice and help you advance your career, the better your chances of success will be.

Some firms may have formal mentoring programs in place, where an experienced attorney serves as a mentor to a new associate. At those firms, new lawyers are assigned to a more seasoned attorney, who may serve several functions: oversee the new lawyer's work product; answer questions; offer ongoing guidance on substantive tasks and other parts of law firm life; provide ongoing training and support to the new attorney; and evaluate the new attorney's work, conduct, and performance for purposes of promotions, compensation, and performance appraisals.

At some firms, formal mentoring programs are structured around practice areas, so, if you're working for the firm's litigation practice group, you may be assigned a mentor who also works in the same practice group. Some firms even set up formal mentoring programs for specific groups of new attorneys: For example, there may be a specific mentoring program for minorities or one for women lawyers.

You won't find formal mentoring programs at every employer. But whether your employer has one or not, perhaps even more important than formal mentoring are the informal, lasting mentoring relationships you should strive to develop as a new lawyer.

One of the most important things you can do on the job during your first year is to find great mentors, believes Janet Hutchinson, Assistant Dean for Career Services at Emory University School of Law. An informal mentor can be available to answer your questions—even those questions you'd consider silly or elementary—and to help you mold and shape your long-term career.

You may find that some mentors will help you with just certain areas or aspects of your career. Consider the following, for example:

- A more experienced colleague at your firm may fill you in on organizational culture and history.

- A third-year associate at another firm whom you meet while working on a case may give you advice on time management and balancing your work and your life.

- A senior associate at your firm may give you guidance on how to complete certain substantive tasks and projects.

- A partner at your firm may answer your questions about timekeeping, billing, and how much time you should be spending on various tasks.

- A former professor or law school administrator may help you pinpoint avenues of employment you may not have considered.

- A seasoned attorney with whom you strike up a conversation at a networking event may help you plan your career next steps.

No matter the type of mentoring you're receiving, it's important that you're receiving it from a source who's not only knowledgeable and experienced, but also able to put you at ease and offer you collegial and congenial advice. The following is a list of qualities that you should look for in a mentor:

- Experience. Your mentor should have work or life experience in the area in which he or she is mentoring you. Note that your mentor doesn't necessarily have to be a seasoned legal professional: Sometimes you may benefit from the insights of another young attorney who's just a year or two ahead of you on the curve. Look for mentors whom you define as successful, says Hutchinson—whatever success means to you, look to team up with more seasoned lawyers and others who have already reached some of the same goals that you've set for yourself.

A mentor in practice, especially one in the lawyer's workplace, can provide valuable insight and interpret the sometimes scattered and confusing information that comes from lawyers further up the chain of command, says Dean David Logan of Roger Williams University School of Law. This is especially important because many senior lawyers are poor managers who fail to give the kind of full information that enables a young lawyer to grasp what is actually expected from a given assignment or then fail at the pedagogic opportunities or "teachable moments" that follow completion of an assignment, Dean Logan explains. A mentor can provide invaluable context in such circumstances and even in some cases serve as an advocate, raising topics with the senior lawyers that seem awkward or even dangerous for the junior lawyer to raise.

- Knowledge to impart. Mentees seek out mentors mainly because mentors possess some knowledge from which mentees can benefit. Make sure all of your mentors have something valuable to share with you—whether it's information about finding meaningful work projects or information about performing various work projects.

- Chemistry. Every mentoring relationship must come with some give and take, and it's important that both mentor and mentee be comfortable in the relationship. You should look for mentors with whom you "click:" Someone to whom you can freely express your thoughts, concerns, and questions. You should be able to have candid conversations with your mentors, says Hutchinson. By that same token, you also have to choose mentors who make you comfortable enough to accept advice and even constructive criticism from that person.

- Understanding. Along the same lines, you should make sure your mentor can empathize or at least sympathize with what you're going through—either because the mentor has already gone through it or because he or she has some understanding of what your life as a new lawyer is like.

- The willingness to teach or mentor. Mentoring takes time, effort, and energy, and not everyone can manage to offer the kind of commitment required during a successful mentoring relationship. Moreover, some people just aren't equipped to teach—they may be successful in their own right, but have trouble relaying advice to others. Make sure the mentors you establish a relationship with are there for you because they want to be.

  Still, understand any limits that your mentors may have, and understand what they're willing to commit to in the mentoring relationship, says Hutchinson. For example, don't ask your mentor questions about a particular topic with which your mentor is not familiar or not comfortable talking about.

- A network. One valuable added benefit to having a mentor is the potential to get to know and network with the mentor's professional network. Look for mentors who are involved in the legal community and also have outside interests, says Hutchinson. A mentor who offers to introduce you to his or her colleagues and professional contacts can provide you with a valuable leg up over other new attorneys who don't have the opportunity to meet those contacts.

That said, you may not always have the opportunity to pick and choose your mentors, and you should always keep an open mind to being mentored by people from all walks of life who may have something valuable to teach or offer you. Take every opportunity to receive quality mentoring, advice, and guidance, both on and off the job. For example, don't discount your law school as a great potential source for you to meet mentors, says Araujo. See if your law school runs a formal mentoring program or a formal referral program; even if it doesn't, your career services office can help introduce you to other alumni or allow you to gain access to alumni, who may be able to provide you with invaluable information about getting started in law practice.

REVEALED!

"I would describe those relationships [with superiors] as mutually respectful and productive. I chose my job primarily based on who my boss would be—and luckily my first impression was accurate: My boss was a great mentor.... The most rewarding part of my work with Ms. JD is the women I meet. It is my job to connect experienced high-achieving attorneys with a community of young aspiring lawyers through our Web site. Talking to women of high achievement is extremely inspiring. Helping young women like me define and achieve success is very satisfying."

Jessie Kornberg, executive director of Ms. JD and 2007 UCLA Law graduate

---

Questions to Ask Your Mentors

At a loss for words when it comes to what you should ask your mentors? The following list can start you in the right direction.

Topic: Working on a Particular Task

- How does this task fit into the firm's overall plans and goals for this case/transaction?

- What is my specific role in executing this task?

- What specific instructions can you give me about executing the task that you think would be important to impart?

- How long should I be spending on this task?

- To whom should I turn for guidance if I have a question?

- What other advice could you offer me before I get started?

Topic: Working in a Practice Area

- What are some of your daily job duties and responsibilities?

- What are some typical tasks that you work on?

- What made you choose this particular area of law?

- How did you get hired in your current position?

- What are some of the most rewarding parts of your job?

- What are some of the greatest challenges that you face?

- What advice would you offer a new lawyer who's interested in working in this area?

Topic: Time Management and Finding Balance

- What does balance mean to you?

- What are some ways that you've become more productive on the job?

- What common time-wasters have you found in your practice, and how were you able to overcome them?

- In what ways do you ensure that you maintain balance between work and the rest of your life?

- How do you know when your balance has been thrown off-kilter, and what do you do to try to prevent that from happening?

Topic: Organizational Culture and History

- What five words would you use to describe the firm?

- How would you describe the firm's mission?

- What do the firm's partners look for in new associates?

- What are some of the things (conduct, behavior, etc.) to avoid on the job at the firm?

- Who are some of the people at the firm that I should get to know, and why?

- Who are some of the people at the firm that I could turn to for advice, guidance, and mentoring?

Topic: Overall Career Goals and Advancement

- What do you consider your greatest career success(es)?

- What is one thing you know now that you wish you had known before you started out as a new attorney?

- Is there anything about your career journey that you would do differently in hindsight?

- What is the most important piece of career advice that you'd like to impart to new lawyers?

Summation

- Expect that the first year on the job will make for a difficult transition and come with a steep learning curve — anticipate some of the greatest challenges that you may face during the first year, read up on them, get guidance, and find ways to handle and cope with them.

- Learn as much as you can on the job.

- Ask lots of questions, be willing to learn new things, and present an eager and positive attitude when taking on new projects.

- Follow up on projects that you've completed.

- Seek out opportunities for professional development, including substantive continuing legal education, practical skills training, business skills training, ethics education, social skills training, and career development.

- Aim to develop long-lasting, quality relationships with mentors.

Homework

- Make a list of the mentors you've had in your life. Next to each person's name, write down at least three things you've learned from that person. Then, write down the qualities that made that person a great mentor.

  Look at your list and come up with at least five new things that you'd like to learn more about as a new lawyer. Then, list potential mentors — these may be current colleagues, professors or administrators, past employers, or simply lawyers whom you met in the past — who could offer you guidance.

- Browse your state's continuing legal education organization's Web site. Pick out at least three upcoming
  conferences, seminars, or other CLE opportunities that
  look interesting or are relevant to what you want to do
  in your career. Do the same thing on the Web site of
  a trade association for lawyers (such as the American
  Intellectual Property Law Association or the Association
  for Corporate Counsel) and a local, state, or national
  bar association (such as the American Bar Association
  or your state's Women's Bar Association). Even if you
  choose not to attend any of the seminars, it will benefit
  you to be aware of the opportunities for professional
  development that are available to you.

CHAPTER 8

GETTING MEANINGFUL ASSIGNMENTS

How can first-year associates lobby for meaningful assignments and make the most of the assignments they are given? This chapter offers tips.

Getting Assignments: How Does It Work?

With today's young lawyer, doing meaningful, interesting work and finding a work-life balance is very important, as is having training and professional development, says Trisha Fillbach, Director of Career Development at Drake Law School. While some law grads may say salary is most important, when it comes down to it, most young lawyers want to do work that interests them.

But getting that kind of work isn't always easy. For many young lawyers, the first year is spent on assignments that some may consider tedious—for example, endless document review and due diligence work. At some large firms, you may be assigned to a particular practice group or specialty pretty

139

early on, and it may not end up being the practice area of your choice, but rather the practice area in which the firm needs help.

Of course, ANY work during the first year is in a sense good experience: You must be able to take each professional experience and project, learn something valuable from it that you can take with you, and tackle it with the same enthusiasm that you would reserve for work that you consider truly fulfilling.

Understand that you won't always like the tasks you are assigned, points out Dean Richard Matasar of New York Law School—after all, it's called "work" for a reason! Even when you're assigned work projects that aren't necessarily fun but are necessary, you must do what's in the best interests of your firm or organization and handle those projects thoroughly, diligently, and effectively, says Matasar.

As soon as you are hired, you should ensure that you know how the process of getting, working on, completing, and getting feedback on assignments works at the firm. You should have clear answers to the following questions:

- Who is responsible for assigning me work?

- What types of projects will I be working on, generally?

- Where can I find samples of documents that I'll be working on?

- What kinds of deadlines will I be working with, generally?

- Where do I get initial guidance on assignments when they are first assigned to me?

- Will I receive a set of instructions with each project, or will I be responsible for figuring out how to perform each task?

- Will I have formal training on each project before I'm assigned a new task, or will I be responsible for researching how to perform each task?

- Where can I find continued guidance if I get stuck on a particular part of a project or need help?

- Who's responsible for overseeing my work?

- To whom do I turn in my assignments?

- Where do I turn for formal or informal feedback on my completed assignments?

Be ready to hit the ground running. At many jobs as a new lawyer, you must be prepared for receiving assignments (sometimes complicated ones) pretty much as soon as you are hired! Many stories abound of young law grads who were asked to argue a motion in court or meet with clients within the first few days (even hours) on the job!

REVEALED!

"I was sworn in on Monday to the Bar and I got a call to come into the DA's office for an interview on Wednesday. I started on Thursday with my [first] plea."

Greg Benoit, Worcester County Assistant District Attorney and 2007 Massachusetts School of Law graduate

Ways to Show Your Abilities

- Offer to take on additional projects. The more you work, the more you learn, believes Rachel Littman, Assistant Dean for Career Development at Pace Law School. Be available, be caring, and demonstrate that you are able to take on more and handle what you're given, and your supervisors will pay attention to your skills and abilities as a result.

- It may sound elementary, but work hard! When new associates don't pull their weight and work diligently, that really irritates senior lawyers, says Littman. Never find yourself doing nothing—ask for more work if you feel that you can handle it, and you won't be caught by surprise by a supervising attorney asking why you didn't bill enough hours last month.

- Show energy and enthusiasm, says Fillbach. Having enthusiasm and energy for your work, your co-workers, and your life in general is infectious and important in helping new associates meet their goals. As Fillbach puts it, no one wants to work with Debbie Downer, the "Saturday Night Live" character. Having enthusiasm and initiative to seek work or volunteer to help a colleague shows a new associate's interest in being a team player and in being a productive member of their office, she adds.

- In fact, you should show enthusiasm for the task at hand no matter how apparently uninteresting it may be, says Dean David Logan of Roger Williams University School of Law. Even if the matter appears boring or inconsequential, a good lawyer uses the assignment to hone and then display his or her technical lawyering skills, Dean Logan says—as he paraphrases an old saying, "If you are a dishwasher, then be the world's best damn dishwasher."

Beginning lawyers, especially at big firms, should be prepared to work on the least exciting parts of huge, complex matters, and it is for the junior lawyer to dive in and work as if the work involved defending a client on death row, says Dean Logan. Even if the matter lacks intrinsic interest or great social value, a beginning lawyer must be sure to display the highest aspects of the lawyers' craft: thorough research, careful analysis of the facts and the law, and a final product that is presented in a crisp and clear manner.

As a first-year associate who's learning the ropes, you simply cannot have a sense of entitlement about being able to pick your projects. You must show the partners that you appreciate all of the opportunities the firm is giving you for learning on the job.

• Also show an eagerness to learn and be open to evaluation (even negative feedback), says Fillbach. Being able to receive and digest constructive criticism shows that you are approaching the job as a professional, that you are constantly striving to improve your work, and that you genuinely care about your employer's feedback and perceptions of your performance.

• Propose new projects when appropriate. Look for pointed projects: Propose new ideas that the firm is currently lacking or ideas that can help the firm with a current project in which the firm is engaged. Be sure to do your homework and research about the project before you propose it.

Approach the right person—a decision-maker who would be interested in hearing about the proposed project—and be prepared with your pitch. Propose the project with the firm in mind: Rather than talk about why you want to take on the new assignment, talk about how the assignment or project will help the firm in the long run. Use terms such as

- "The project will benefit the client by..."

- "The project will increase the firm's visibility by..."

- "The project will potentially allow the firm to cross-market its services by..."

- Try to identify the senior lawyers who are the decision-makers and try to work for them or otherwise come to their attention in a positive way, says Dean Logan. Similarly, some areas of practice are likely to be "hotter" than others, he says: A wise junior lawyer avoids the backwater and rather seeks work in the practice area(s) that generate the largest return for the employer or otherwise seem to be near the center rather than the periphery of the office.

- Don't turn in sloppy work, warns Janet Hutchinson, Assistant Dean for Career Services at Emory University School of Law. Part of being successful is showing that you can successfully complete the projects and tasks that were assigned to you, Hutchinson points out. Being detail-oriented and paying attention to even the most minute details in your work product shows that you take pride in your work.

  Senior attorneys appreciate it when associates turn in client-ready work, Hutchinson explains. Turn in work product that you consider a final version—work that you are happy to have churned out.

- Be clear about expectations before you begin a new work project, communicate as clearly as possible and as often as needed about your assignments, and make sure your supervisors and you are on the same page as far as how you're progressing during the first year, Hutchinson stresses.

- Show as much flexibility as possible when it comes to work assignments, recommends Beverly Bracker, Director of Career Services at Thomas Jefferson School of Law. For example, say you are pulled off of a project on which you've been working for a while—instead of having a negative attitude about it, go with the flow and trust that your employer will give you other opportunities to show your talents.

- Be visible in the office, recommends Mandie Araujo, Director of Career Services at New England Law| Boston. Working hard is a given, but it may not always be enough—you must also make sure that you project that you're part of the team and happy to be there.

  Don't close your door, periodically walk the hallways to say hello to the partners or other people and engage them in conversation, attend firm events outside of work, and show that you're an engaged participant in the firm's everyday work.

Getting Evaluated and Conducting Self-Evaluations

In most firms, associates will likely be formally evaluated periodically by their supervisors. During a formal evaluation, you're gauged on your performance at the firm and the value you bring to the firm. Some of the factors that might be considered during your evaluation include

- Your productivity and billing
- Your skills and abilities in completing assignments
- Your substantive knowledge in law practice

- Your business development skills and the business you've brought into the firm
- Your timeliness and ability to meet deadlines
- Your enthusiasm and attitude
- Your overall fit at the firm

As with anything else, different firms will conduct performance evaluations in various ways. At some firms, you can expect to have several formal evaluations each year, covering your pay raises, promotions, bonuses, considerations for partnership, and overall progress at the firm. Other firms may simply conduct an annual evaluation or may even forego formal evaluations in favor of informal appraisals done periodically by your supervisors.

At some firms, there is a "no news is good news" approach to feedback. (And—although this shouldn't be happening for obvious practical, professional, and ethical reasons—at some busy firms, training, supervision, and evaluations are virtually nonexistent. So be prepared: You may be met with no appraisals or feedback and be left to your own devices when it comes to gauging your performance and progress on the job. In those instances, it's even more important that you conduct periodic self-evaluations.)

You should gauge how your firm or employer handles evaluations and feedback and act accordingly—if feedback is readily provided by your supervisors, then by all means ask for it; if it's scarcely provided unless your work product is deficient, then you may not want to constantly approach the partners about giving you their two cents on how you handled every single project.

Also, remember that you're no longer in law school—grades don't matter in the real world; what matters is that you consistently turn out efficient and high-quality work product, says Matasar. Every new lawyer is expected to churn out high-quality work, and you can't expect a "pat on the back" for doing so, Matasar points out. As a lawyer, you have to learn to produce excellent work all the time, do it efficiently, and do it without much fuss, Matasar explains.

You shouldn't, however, wait to be formally evaluated on the job by your supervisors—it's just as important that you conduct periodic self-evaluations where you take stock in your own professional development and gauge how well you're doing according to your own perceptions. A formal evaluation is a performance appraisal conducted by your employer to track your work product, your performance, and your progress. A self-evaluation is a performance appraisal that you conduct on yourself, evaluating your own work product, performance, and progress on the job.

When you're conducting a self-evaluation, appraise your skills and your performance by asking the same questions and evaluating the same factors as your employer would use during a formal evaluation. Be sure to be honest with yourself during a self-evaluation: The point is to gauge your performance as accurately as possible, figure out your strengths and weaknesses, and discern what areas and skills you still need to work on.

It may also be helpful to keep a formal "career journal," particularly during that all-important first year on the job as a new lawyer. The career journal serves various purposes: It helps you keep track of the work you've done; note important milestones in your career; pinpoint your strengths and weaknesses; track your progress at work in detail; and serve as a reference point during evaluations, self-evaluations, questions from your supervisor about your work, and even billing and timekeeping.

Your career journal should include the following things:

- Assignments, tasks, and projects you have worked on, including dates of assignment and dates of completion

- Detailed information about any awards, accomplishments, and achievements

- Details about any compliments, critiques, or constructive criticism you receive on the job

- Your periodically updated resume

- Information about any continuing legal education or professional development you attend

- Information about any formal and informal training or mentoring you receive on the job

- The assessment and outcomes of your evaluations and self-evaluations

- Detailed information about your referrals, business development practices, potential client leads, and other pitches

- Detailed information about any instance where you went above and beyond your call of duty to assist or serve your employer

Summation

- As soon as you are hired, become familiar with the firm's process of assigning work, completing projects, and getting feedback on completed work.

- Don't be afraid to ask for meaningful assignments: Offer to take on additional assignments; propose a new project that will help the firm; and show energy, enthusiasm, and initiative.

- Be flexible when it comes to getting and completing assignments.

- Turn in work product that you consider "client-ready:" work that makes you feel proud and that you consider to be a final product.

- Never sit idly: Show your value to your employer by handling your assigned projects well and then helping out with additional assignments.

- Ask for periodic feedback and evaluations, and conduct self-evaluations to keep track of your progress at the firm.

- Consider keeping a "career journal" to keep track of your career progress in detail.

Homework

- Put together an evaluation form that you would use to evaluate a new lawyer's work during the first year on the job. What categories might you include? What character traits would you look for? How would you measure the employee's productivity and value to the firm? How would you ascertain that the employee is doing his or her job well? What would you like to be evaluated on as a first-year associate?

  Here are some general categories you may wish to include—make up questions or evaluation points for each, along with any additional categories that you may deem important:

- Business development skills
- Performance on assigned tasks
- Productivity
- Receptiveness to feedback
- Timeliness and ability to meet deadlines
- Billing
- Substantive knowledge
- Practical skills
- Attitude and enthusiasm
- Interactions with clients, peers, supervisors, and others
- Fit

CHAPTER 9

INCREASING YOUR MARKETABILITY AND BUILDING YOUR CLIENT BASE

W hat are some of the skills and techniques that you must learn and hone as a new lawyer to help you with business development? This chapter tells you.

What Must You Know About Making Yourself More Marketable?

First and foremost, you have to know well and understand your work and the work of your firm. It isn't enough to have a general understanding of your firm's business, services, and mission—you must be able to answer some questions that existing and potential clients may raise, and you must preferably have a "sound bite" ready to go to convey to those clients essential information about your work and the work of your firm that will put you in the best light possible.

For example, you have to have a good handle on the following concepts:

- How your law firm operates

- What your partners and supervising attorneys want

- What skills your firm considers essential in its associates

- What services and niches your firm offers

- What your firm's mission is

- What your firm's business model is and what its business goals are

- What some of the attorneys' greatest accomplishments are

- What differentiates your firm from others

- What aspects of your firm—and your own work—are most salable to potential and existing clients

But knowing your own firm is not enough, points out Ari Kaplan, principal at Ari Kaplan Advisors. You also have to know what your clients want and how you can best provide what they want, and you have to understand the legal environment and how your own firm fits into the landscape. As Kaplan puts it, many new lawyers can do research or review documents, but those lawyers who add value—by demonstrating an ability to both do the work and consider the key concerns of the clients and the lawyers at the firm—will stand out, even in a stagnant economy. So, Kaplan says, young lawyers must understand the industry landscape by studying the environment in which they are working and the individuals with whom they are associated.

For example, you must know

- Who your clients are

- What your clients are seeking from you and your firm

- What corporate law departments and other clients want and how they operate, generally

- How your firm fits into the legal landscape

- Who the players are in the legal landscape

- How to best use the media in marketing your firm and your services

- How to best use social networking in marketing your firm and your services

- How to best market your firm and services in person

- How your firm fits into your major clients' lives and business models

- How your firm stands out among others

- What makes your clients choose your firm and bring you continued business

In addition, you have to be familiar with all of the formal and informal marketing efforts your firm undertakes. It is not enough to know that there are lawyers and clients, Kaplan explains: There are lawyers, there are clients, there are support services, there are experts within firms, there are experts outside of firms, there are companies that create products for the legal industry—the list goes on. Kaplan says a new lawyer must know all of these different aspects in order to develop marketing savvy.

For example, you should know

- What formal marketing materials (such as brochures and booklets) are available for your use at the firm

- What's on your firm's Web site, where (and in what ways) your firm appears on the Internet, and when information about your firm is updated online

- What publications and other outlets your firm advertises in

- How your firm handles published articles written by the firm's lawyers

- Who at your firm is considered an expert in a specific area(s) and what it takes to become an expert in an area

- Who at your firm is in charge of marketing efforts and how they can assist you with marketing your own services

Why Is It Essential for New Lawyers to Begin Building Their Books of Business as Soon as Possible?

During the first year, it's easy to get stuck in the mountain of work you have to get through each day and forget about making time for business development, points out Jeff Catalano, a Boston partner in the law firm of Todd and Weld who often speaks about business development to lawyers and legal professionals. Plus, new associates may be ambivalent about business development because they lack confidence or don't know how to approach a potential client, Catalano says.

But like building your network, building your book of business takes lots of time and trust, which must be built up over time, Kaplan and Catalano both point out. Bringing in business—even better, continued business—is one surefire way to impress your partners and show your value to the firm. And a client base can take many years to develop, says Kaplan, so the longer you wait to get started, the longer it will take for you to build it up.

Plus, many legal employers nowadays are looking for young lawyers to hit the ground running—not just when it comes to substantive knowledge and work product, but also when it comes to building the firm's client base. In particular, if you are working for a smaller firm, you may be expected to bring in business as soon as you start your first year. As a result, it's vital that you learn some of the skills and techniques that will help you with business development.

Every new lawyer must understand how to raise his or her profile by helping to raise the profile of others, says Kaplan. He adds that new lawyers must be genuinely enthusiastic about the work and potential work they are doing—pursuing areas within your list of passions and doing things that excite you, he says, will help you become more marketable and develop your book of business.

> ## REVEALED!
>
> "I am even networking in my sleep. Nearly all of my clients are based on referrals. For me, every meeting is a chance to meet two to three neat individuals. Usually, I strive to meet individuals who are gatekeepers for meeting a handful of clients. I am part of at least two full-time networking groups with regular meetings and attendance. After a while, the folks in the networking group kind of become like a second family."
>
> *Amir Atashi Rang, principal of The Atashi Rang Law Firm and 2000 UC Hastings graduate*

Business Development Tips for Young Lawyers

- Exude confidence. The first year can be the most difficult for new graduates, especially those who went to law school right after receiving their undergraduate degrees, because of their age, says Trisha Fillbach, Director of Career Development at Drake Law School. Many new attorneys, especially younger attorneys, are not always taken seriously because they appear too young—Fillbach says she has had graduates tell her that their clients do not take them as seriously as they should because of the color of their hair or the sound of their voice, and she has even experienced this as a new attorney herself.

  The lack of experience for some graduates can cause a decrease in self-confidence. In addition, very few, if any, graduates coming out of law school have a "book of business," or built-in client base. Most larger firms do not expect new associates to bring in new business immediately, but some smaller firms do, and for a sole practitioner it is imperative that you not only practice law but also market yourself. The best way to overcome this, Fillbach says, is by knowing your area of the law and exhibiting confidence while counseling those clients.

- Learn from the pros. Ask your partners to take you with them to business development meetings, says Catalano. Observe how the partners "make the pitch," describe the firm, or sell the firm's attorneys. Watch the partners for pointers and adopt the business development techniques that you find most successful to use on your own, Catalano advises.

  If you don't feel comfortable approaching a potential new client on your own, consider bringing a partner with you, Catalano offers: You'll learn about business development from the partner, bond/network with the partner, and also convey to the partner that business development is important to you.

- Stay up to date on your field. Keep track of trends and changes in your industry or practice area, recommends Lisa Terrizzi, career coach and consultant and chairperson of the Massachusetts Bar Association's Lawyers in Transition Committee. Read up on ongoing trends and happenings in trade journals and join professional associations to ensure you stay in the loop about changes, best practices, and ways to best serve your clients or services to offer to potential new clients.

- Know your clients, understand their business and their wants, and understand how you can best serve those needs with your work. Just as any product manufacturer worth his or her salt will know his or her clients and the product inside and out, you must know well the services you provide, the clients you serve, and how your work fits into the client's life or business. Lawyers who demonstrate marketability can genuinely convey to their clients and their communities what they do and how they do it, Kaplan points out.

- Think in broad terms, says Kaplan: Senior lawyers want their junior associates to think about clients and business development matters in a broad way and to consider the impact of their work and their pitches on the "big picture," he adds.

- Portray the right image: You have to "be" a partner before you can become a partner, says Catalano. That means you have to think like partners do about business development and show an inclination, desire, and ability to generate business for the firm. It also means that you have to be cognizant of the business aspect of practicing law, Catalano adds, and grasp the idea of selling your time. Partners invest in associates, says Catalano, and they make a return when the associate works hard and keeps close track of time, leading to profit realized from the associate's efforts.

- Be prepared when you make your pitch. Know what you're going to say or show before you meet with the potential client, research the client's needs and preferences, and prepare a thorough and well-thought-out presentation to the extent possible. Be assertive but professional about making your approach, says Catalano, and portray that you're comfortable in your own skin.

Summation

- Begin building your book of business as soon as you are hired—remember that building a client base takes time, effort, and trust.

- Familiarize yourself with your firm's formal and informal marketing efforts, advertising, and business development.

- Be familiar with your firm's attorneys, services, and mission and understand what makes your firm stand out from the rest.

- Be familiar with who your clients are, what your clients need and want, and how you can best serve your clients' needs.

- Be familiar with the legal landscape and understand how your firm fits into that landscape.

- Project a confident and self-assured image to clients, potential clients, partners, and others.

- Present pointed and well-thought-out pitches when you're asking for new business.

Homework

- Think of some of the qualities and skills you possess that make you stand out from other candidates for employment and make a list of them. Then, write a 30-second pitch that you might make to a potential employer if you were trying to highlight some of your best qualities and practice it on someone whose opinion you trust.

- Next, make a list of potential "clients" (including people you know and people you may want to get to know) to whom you might market those same qualities. As this is just an exercise, you don't have to follow up with those people, of course—the idea is for you to write a focused pitch and then brainstorm the names of people who might listen to it.

- Study the business model of a law firm you admire. How does the firm work to develop its business? What skills and techniques does it employ? What qualities does it highlight to clients and potential clients when it comes to the firm's attorneys and services?

CHAPTER 10

INCREASING YOUR PRODUCTIVITY—AND YOUR BILLING

T his chapter offers advice for increasing your productivity during your first year, as well as bettering your billing and business development skills.

Common Productivity Pitfalls—and Ways to Avoid Them

One common mistake young lawyers make is saying yes to everything—only to find out that they can't do it all, says Rachel Littman, Assistant Dean for Career Development at Pace Law School. Although maintaining a busy schedule and full workload is essential to impress legal employers, new lawyers have to figure out how much time needs to be spent on each task (realistically) and take on only as much as they can handle. Remember: The ethics rules demand that attorneys perform competent work for their clients. If you're biting off more than you can chew, you won't be performing as competently as possible.

Keeping contemporaneous notes, diligently marking your start and end times on projects, setting realistic deadlines, and meeting those deadlines are all skills that are essential for young lawyers to learn, Littman adds. Not being productive on the job can really irritate supervising lawyers, she says. It's important that young lawyers show their supervisors how hard they are willing to work during the first year on the job and beyond.

You may also be less productive if you lack a concrete plan or schedule for your workday, as well as for each individual assignment that you begin, says Kelly Anders, Associate Dean for Student Affairs at Washburn University School of Law and author of *The Organized Lawyer* (Carolina Academic Press, 2009).

In some cases, first-year associates may also lack the confidence needed to ask questions about beginning a project, which can make for wasted time. You must be comfortable with where you are going with each project and ask the questions you need to have answered in order to get the project started faster, says Anders.

Another common time-waster? Not doing things right the first time around. If you're consistently finding yourself going back to completed assignments in order to correct your own mistakes, double-check details, or fix sloppy work, you are wasting time and probably not being as productive as you could be. For the sake of efficiency, aim to do things right the first time and double-check your final work product.

Finally, you may also be less productive if you fail to delegate tasks when appropriate, Anders points out. Make sure that you're not spending valuable time doing things that other people could be doing for you, Anders says, particularly if your time is more valuable spent elsewhere. For example, it may seem like a luxury, but consider delegating your dry cleaning or meal-making to someone else, Anders says: The time you save may be better spent on your practice or even simply on relaxing and taking some time out for yourself. At work, make sure you're delegating projects to the lowest level possible— spend your time on a task that requires your attention rather than on tasks that you could delegate to your support staff.

Remember that the concept of productivity encompasses both subjective and objective ideals and definitions. The best indicator of productivity is having reached the goals that you have set for yourself, Anders says. Just be sure that your ideals of productivity match or surpass the ideals of productivity that your supervisors and your employers have in place, says Anders—having surpassed the firm's concepts of what constitutes efficient work is a sure indicator that you are a productive employee.

REVEALED!

"I think everyone spends a part of the first year facing the hard truth that no matter how hard you worked in law school, working a 9 to 5 (or an 8 to 10) is hard, exhausting, and not nearly as much fun as being in school…. I'm very organized (I'm all about lists and checking things off them)—and that was crucial in a job with a lot going on and a fair amount of autonomy."

Jessie Kornberg, executive director of Ms. JD and 2007 UCLA Law graduate

A Productivity Checklist: Pinpointing Your Productivity Strengths and Weaknesses

Before you can begin to increase your productivity, you must understand what you do efficiently and where you may have some room for improvement. Consider the following checklist and answer the following questions honestly to gauge how efficient and productive you are on and off the job:

- Do you start every day or every new project with a clear plan for what you need to do and by when you need to complete each task?

- On most days, do you complete all or most of the tasks that are on your to-do list?

- Do you meet each and every deadline that is set for you or that you've set for yourself?

- Do you consistently take longer than you should on any particular type of task or project?

- Do you have any particular habits that prevent you from being efficient—are you the victim of any of the common "time-wasters" listed earlier?

- Do you delegate tasks and projects efficiently whenever appropriate?

- Do you ever find yourself going back to a previously completed task that you did not do properly the first time around?

- Do you have a clear idea of what your firm or employer expects of you in terms of productivity and efficiency?

- Do your ideals of productivity and efficiency match or surpass the expectations of your firm or employer?

- Compare yourself to your colleagues and peers (and even your supervisors) in terms of productivity: Are you on par with the rest of the firm when it comes to efficiency, or are you any more or less efficient than most of the lawyers at your firm?

Billing Tips for Young Lawyers

- Remember that you will be expected to bill your time as soon as you are hired. Your time is the stock of your trade: As a lawyer, you don't deal in "widgets" or products; you deal in hours.

- Be clear about your firm's expectations regarding billing, time-keeping, and billable hours. Understand how many hours you are supposed to bill (or aim to bill) and recognize that not everything you do can be billed out to clients; plan accordingly.

- Learn to keep meticulous track of your time. Hone your time management skills and keep detailed timesheets.

- Stay clear of any unscrupulous billing practices, such as padding your timesheets or double-billing.

- Be as specific as possible when it comes to your timesheets. Don't just jot down the name of the client whose case you worked on; write down the task you performed in enough detail that if you're asked about what you did down the line, you are able to give a clear answer.

- Practice "billing" your time before you're even hired— perhaps as part of your job search, or even while you prepare for the bar exam. For every task that you work on as part of the job search—for example, updating your resume or meeting a potential employer—write down in detail the nature of the task, the time you spent on it, the date and time you performed it, and any notes that should accompany your entry.

Summation

- To be a valuable employee, you must aim to be efficient and productive.

- Approach each and every day—and every new project and assignment—with a clear plan for where you are going.

- Avoid common time-wasters, such as not delegating work when appropriate or not doing a project right the first time around.

- Use technology, legal staff, and time management tools to your advantage and make them work for you—ultimately making you more efficient.

- Keep meticulous track of your time and billing.

- Understand your firm's expectations when it comes to billing, keeping track of your time, and billable hours.

Homework

- Complete the productivity checklist in this chapter. Then come up with a concrete plan for five ways that you will aim to increase your productivity. Reduce your plan to writing.

- Practice "billing" your time while you're looking for your first job. Write down the precise amount of time you're spending on career planning, job searching, and related tasks.

CHAPTER 11

BUILDING YOUR NETWORK

T he value of networking is tremendous, especially when you're learning the ropes as a new lawyer. This chapter offers networking tips for new lawyers.

What Does Networking Mean?

To me, networking means establishing, building, and cultivating long-lasting professional relationships. Networking takes many shapes and forms. For example, I feel that I am effectively networking when I

- Attend a continuing legal education seminar and meet like-minded lawyers who are also seeking to improve their skill set and niche

- Send along a quick e-mail to another legal professional with a link to an article that I think may interest that person

- Speak at a conference to other lawyers or legal professionals and then take a few minutes to make conversation with a group of them after the conference

169

- Volunteer to serve on the board of trustees of my son's school

- Tell my family or circle of friends about my upcoming books

- Update my professional profile, all the while checking the profiles of people in my network to see who in my professional network may need to be congratulated on good news

- Send a handwritten thank-you note to a person whom I interviewed for an article

- Send clients my e-mail newsletter, in which I provide tips and advice as well as updates about my services

- Subscribe to a Google feed or online newsletter of the firms at which I have professional contacts in order to get breaking news and current events about those firms and their lawyers

- Share a tip with my network online

One thing that's essential is that both individuals get something out of the professional relationship in which they are engaged, according to the experts. Networking means creating and developing relationships in which both individuals provide and receive value from the connection, says Ari Kaplan, author of *The Opportunity Maker: Strategies for Inspiring Your Legal Career Through Networking and Business Development* and principal at Ari Kaplan Advisors. Networking, Kaplan says, is a two-way street: It is based on a genuine foundation of interest and appreciation for one another. In fact, Kaplan says that networking is often about showcasing who you are through the actions you take to help others promote their own efforts, all of which will reflect positively on your character.

Think of networking as just another way to establish new relationships and cultivate existing ones. Aim to develop a human bond before you develop a professional bond, says Jeff Catalano, partner in the Boston office of Todd & Weld, LLP, who speaks frequently about networking and business development to lawyers.

So, don't think of networking as this awkward activity—this notion that networking gets done while uncomfortably talking about the weather at a cocktail party with people whom you barely know or seeking out people just for the purpose of schmoozing them for business or professional advancement.

In fact, it may pay off not to think of networking as "networking" at all: Because the concept of "networking" gets a reputation as this uncomfortable activity, you are better off thinking of cultivating your relationships simply for the sake of cultivating your relationships. In other words, approach each person for the sake of making a human connection—not just for the sake of making a professional connection that may potentially influence your career. Don't expect to get anything specific (like a job offer or an introduction to a particular person) out of networking with someone; doing so will just put undue pressure on you. Rather, expect to simply make a human bond with your professional contact.

Networking Tips for the New Lawyer

- First and foremost, do it! The more you affirmatively take the time to network, the more comfortable you'll be doing it, says Catalano. For many young lawyers, time constraints (as in just trying to get all their work done in the limited time they have) can often mean that networking takes a back seat to time in the office—and in some cases is completely lost in the shuffle. Still, making time to spend with professional contacts is important, Catalano says: Professional bonds take years to develop, and it's important that you begin developing them early in your career.

- Every time you meet someone new and have a conversation with that person, be sure to remember something from that conversation, says Kaplan. One good trick? Take the person's business card and write down a few words that you remember from your conversation to help you jog your memory about that person the next time you see or talk to each other—then, use the piece of information you've jotted down in your next conversation to show genuine interest in that person. For example, if you meet a litigator who tells you that she's working on a big products liability case, follow up and ask how the case was resolved.

- Keep people involved in and informed about your career. Remember that client relationships and relationships with supervisors are based on trust, long-term relationships, and your capability, says Kaplan. He adds that many people enjoy watching a new lawyer grow and transform throughout his or her career. So, let your mentor know about your accomplishments; include your clients in your newsletter (unless, of course, they opt out of receiving it); and don't be afraid to build trust and lasting relationships by periodically revealing what you're working on, what you're looking for, and where you are in your career.

Don't wait for an invitation to call: People do want those unexpected phone calls or e-mails if they have some merit behind them, says Kaplan, so don't be afraid to share a pointed question, an interesting story, or a congratulatory gesture.

- Also share your own stories, says Catalano. Come up with an interesting story that illustrates what you do: for example, a fascinating case that you worked on. Share that story when someone asks you what you do. And most importantly, love what you do and let people know that you love what you do, Catalano says.

- Experiment with different opportunities and environments for networking and go with interactions that feel comfortable to you, says Kaplan. He adds that there are unlimited places where lawyers can network: The golf course or basketball court, continuing legal education seminars, and charitable or nonprofit work are just some examples.

- Having an organized approach to networking is the best way to go about networking, says Trisha Fillbach, Director of Career Development at Drake Law School. When you meet new people, follow up with them. Create a Rolodex—either electronic or paper—and keep track of new contacts.

  If you meet people in an industry you practice in, send them articles you think they may be interested in or let them know about an upcoming seminar on a topic relevant to their work. Overall, be open to meeting new people, sharing ideas, and keeping track of the contacts you develop through networking and following up with them, says Fillbach.

- If you're uncomfortable with networking or meeting people, Kaplan recommends that you experiment with starting conversations, adding that those who are uncomfortable with networking often have trouble engaging others in conversation as well. Kaplan recommends first asking people what they do and why they enjoy it and then following up with additional questions and conversation based on the person's answers.

- Recognize your own value in networking with others, says Kaplan. Don't just gauge a potential professional contact by the value he or she can provide to you and your career; rather, understand and recognize the value you can provide to others when you network with them. Understanding what you bring to the table will allow you to be not only more confident but also more comfortable communicating with others and establishing relationships.

- Keep the networking ball rolling. Kaplan recommends introducing people in your network to each other. He says that when you introduce someone to another individual who you feel is an interesting person for him or her to meet, you not only demonstrate your generosity in opening up your network, but you also highlight your thoughtfulness.

- A huge part of networking: following up, both Kaplan and Catalano say. For example, when you refer a potential client to a lawyer acquaintance, follow up with both sources as part of your networking efforts. When you conduct an informational interview with a potential employer or take a lawyer friend out for coffee to ask him about practicing in his field, send a thank-you note. Periodically, send along some pointed and pertinent information (like a timely article or news brief) to contacts who may be interested in reading it.

In other words, once you make a professional bond with someone, don't just drop off the face of the planet. Follow up and keep maintaining and nurturing that bond through frequent or periodic professional interactions.

REVEALED!

"Our relationships are all we have. It is important to culti-vate and manage your relationships. Keeping a database is mandatory—whether it's through e-mail or any other elec-tronic database. I personally use Microsoft Outlook."

Nikon Limberis, equity trader and 2007 New York Law School graduate

Tips for Approaching Lawyers and Legal Professionals (Even If You Don't Know Them)

I know, I know: Some young lawyers say they'd feel more comfortable gouging out their own eyeballs than networking and approaching lawyers and legal professionals whom they don't know very well—or at all! But meeting new people in the profession doesn't have to be full of pressure.

- First, don't think you have to go looking for someone new in order to network. Tap your existing network— your friends, family, fellow students, professors, business associates, and anyone else you know professionally— and start talking them up. Ask them to introduce you to other professionals. You'd be surprised by how many great new contacts you can make this way—after all, almost everyone knows a lawyer!

- Take the focus off of you, and focus on the work instead. For example, instead of focusing on what you can tell a potential employer about your skills or interests, start by telling the potential employer about an article you read that may be of interest. Then, let your common interest in that subject lead to a conversation about your professional interests and skills.

- Have one foolproof question that you can pose to someone you'd like to meet. Ask, for example, "What do you do?" or "What made you choose the legal profession?" By beginning the conversation with a question rather than an introduction or a comment, you open up a chance for dialogue.

  When the person answers your question, take the opportunity to introduce yourself. Extend your hand and say your full name. In most cases, the person will introduce himself or herself, and in many cases, he or she will ask you a question in return as well, in which case you can take the opportunity to keep the dialogue flowing.

- Stay engaged in your conversations. When the person tells you something interesting, make a mental note of it and ask a follow-up question about it. For example, when the person tells you that he or she works in a particular practice group or practice area, ask what the most challenging part of working in that field is, or ask the person to share an interesting case on which he or she worked in the past.

- Go alone to networking events, recommends Mandi Araujo, Director of Career Services at New England Law|Boston. If you go with a friend, you will be more likely to stick to each other's presence during the event and less likely to meet new people—including potential employers. Go solo and aim to introduce yourself to people at the event.

- Aim for quality, not quantity, says Catalano. Set a goal for yourself. For example, aim to meet three new people at one event and really strike up a conversation with them, as opposed to shaking lots of hands and coming away with the feeling that you didn't truly meet anyone new. Have your "sound bites" ready so that when you're asked a question about your work or your career, you provide a succinct and eloquent answer instead of stumbling around looking for the right words to use.

- Make face time at events where you already know people. For example, attend charity events or pro bono programs at which your firm buys a table, Catalano says. Start by attending your own firm's events, where you'll already know some people who may then be able to introduce you to others you can add to your professional network. Alternatively, attend charitable events at a nonprofit you are familiar with—or even alumni events organized by your law school.

- Don't just stick to the legal field. Join cross-industry associations and approach their members for networking as well, says Lisa Terrizzi, career coach and consultant and chairperson of the Massachusetts Bar Association's Lawyers in Transition Committee.

For instance, if you are a labor and employment associate, you should join the Society for Human Resource Management—after all, its members (human resources managers and officers) are your potential clients! Hearing out the concerns of those members can give you valuable insight into the field that you won't get from networking within just the legal field. Plus, meeting people who are at the junior level in that industry will allow you to establish lasting relationships with people who may give you business in the future, Terrizzi points out.

Summation

- Think of networking in terms of human bonds, not just professional bonds.

- Remember that networking is a two-way street: Share information (about your field, your knowledge, your contacts, and yourself) with your network.

- Don't put undue pressure on yourself by expecting that networking with a person will lead to anything specific (like a job offer); rather, network for the sake of establishing, developing, and cultivating professional relationships.

- Experiment with different opportunities and environments for networking.

- Start conversations and stay engaged during them.

- Approach people—as with anything else, the more you network, the more comfortable you'll feel doing it.

- Aim for quality, not quantity, when building your network.

- Follow up with your professional contacts periodically.

Homework

- Take fifteen minutes to write one of your professional contacts a letter, note, or e-mail. As some examples, you could

  - Thank the person for something that he or she has helped you with in your career.

- Introduce the person to another contact whom they may like to meet.

- Forward an interesting article or news brief to the person.

- Share some news about your career development.

- Congratulate the person on some accomplishment or news in his or her career development.

- In the next week, aim to meet three new people in your professional capacity as a new lawyer, law graduate, or law student. Spend enough time talking to each person so that you walk away with the following:

  - Know what the person does professionally.

  - Understand what he or she most enjoys about his or her job.

  - Share at least one of your professional passions or success stories with the person.

  - Take one piece of career advice from the person.

ORGANIZING YOUR WORK AND YOUR LIFE, MANAGING YOUR TIME, AND MANAGING YOUR MONEY

This chapter offers young lawyers advice on three key areas with skills to master on and off the job: organizational skills, time management skills, and financial management.

Tips for Honing Your Organizational Skills

All too often, young lawyers don't realize how important organizational skills are to the practice of law, says Kelly Anders, Associate Dean for Student Affairs at Washburn University School of Law and author of *The Organized Lawyer* (Carolina Academic Press, 2009). There are so many projects and topics coming at a new associate that it may be tempting to think it's best to tackle everything all at once—or without a clear and detailed plan of action. But as a busy and time-pressed young lawyer, if you're not organizing your work, your resources, and your life, you are probably going to decrease your efficiency and be less productive on the job, Anders says.

Adding to the challenge, some firms don't have clear guidelines in place about how attorneys are supposed to organize their files, their projects, their cases, their offices, and their work overall, says Anders. That makes it more difficult for young lawyers to think about organization—after all, without much guidance, where do you even start? Yet, as Anders points out, all of that makes it even more important that you go into the job with a plan and having developed a clear-cut, regimented, and regular system for keeping yourself organized.

It is essential that you have everything in its proper place and know where you can find everything at all times, Anders stresses—not just because spending less time looking for things will make you more efficient, but also because knowing where something is will make you look more professional when someone inevitably pops into your office to inquire about the whereabouts of that document, file, or e-mail message.

As Anders says, this is a non-delegable duty: You must know your own organizational system and can't just rely on your support staff or someone else to design, implement, and maintain it for you!

The following is a list of some of the specific areas of your work and your life that you need to organize and maintain:

- Your filing system. If your firm has in place a clear system for keeping and maintaining files, then be sure you get to know that system throughout and comport with it when you file your own documents and materials. If there is no set system in place, Anders says you must learn to develop your own—an organized way of filing that will keep you efficient.

Among other things, consider what names or titles you'll assign to each file; what system of organization (numerical, alphabetical, or other) you'll adopt; whether you'll color-code your files; whether you'll have a separate file for documents that you're currently working on; what impact your system might have on file-sharing with others; and any other considerations that are pertinent to your work specifically.

- Your computer. Hard-copy files are not the only folders that need to be organized and properly maintained—your electronic files also count. For example, think about what folders you need to set up in order to organize your electronic documents; how you'll handle redlined documents and how you'll share them with the rest of your team; at what time intervals you'll purge; how you'll organize your e-mail account, any e-mail folders, sent e-mail messages, and saved e-mail messages; and any other concerns regarding electronic organization that you encounter on the job.

- Your office space. Design and develop systems in your office (or on your desk) that will make you a more efficient lawyer, says Anders. This may take some time, she says, but will ultimately save you time in the long run. For example, think about where you should position items that you'll be using frequently, what you should keep close at hand and what items you want to display so as to project a professional workspace.

- Your billing and timesheets. Again, if your firm has a particular format that it uses, you should make sure you quickly familiarize yourself with it and adapt it for your use. If not, it's essential that you develop your own detailed and organized system for keeping track of time. Anders recommends that you write down the dates, times of day, and lengths of time that you work on a project; the client name or code; the task you performed or action you took; and sufficient notes to remind you of anything important you or others need to know about that action. (Anders recommends developing letter codes or shorthand for each task or action you may undertake—if your firm doesn't have this in place—to make it easier for you to track your own work and for others to follow what you're doing.)

- Your contact database. Naturally, you need to include contact information in your database for all of your professional contacts, but don't just stop with e-mail addresses and phone numbers: Anders says young lawyers often miss the opportunity to turn their contact databases into a personalized trove of information that may help them with business development and networking.

  Anders recommends making notes about your contacts' preferences or personalizing them with some pertinent information about each contact—that way, you can use your customized database to pitch projects or invite people to events that are in line with their preferences. (For example, you may note that an important client likes baseball, jazz, or art and then may invite that client to business development events that are in line with the client's interests.) Whatever method you choose, make sure you maintain an organized system for keeping up with your contacts.

© JIST Works

- Your wardrobe. Having an organized professional wardrobe will help you look presentable and professional. Anders recommends trying things on in advance before your work week begins and planning your outfits ahead of time so that you can spend less time contemplating what you'll wear and simply get dressed each morning.

- Anything else in your work life that will help you run things more smoothly and efficiently. As one example, you should have several routes to work (or to court, or to that all-important client's headquarters) planned out and plugged into your PDA to help you in case you hit traffic.

You should have an organized attaché case or carrying bag in working order as well, says Anders. You may also want to stock up on personal supplies of items you may need at work (like aspirin or even snacks) to keep from spending valuable time running out for them when you really need them.

The bottom line? Plan for the unexpected, organize everything meticulously, and maintain a regimented and regular system for all areas of your work life.

Time Management Tips for New Lawyers

One thing that every new lawyer wishes he or she had more of? Time! As a new lawyer, you'll undoubtedly be working long hours and late nights, getting hit with assignments that need your immediate and undivided attention. Plus, juggling a busy work schedule with your other commitments can be quite a challenge. As a result, you have to master time management skills to help keep you afloat and succeed at getting everything done on time.

To me, time management is a three-step process:

1. I compartmentalize all of the tasks I have to accomplish during a given day, week, etc. I do this in writing so that I am left with a comprehensive list of everything I need to do, separating them into general headings according to whatever part of my life and my work require my attention.

2. I prioritize all of the tasks I wrote down. This may be as simple as numbering them in order of importance or noting to myself what tasks must be done by a certain date or time.

3. I plan my day or week according to the order of priority I set for each task that I must complete.

The following are some additional tips for time management that you may find useful.

- Set realistic expectations. Understand how long a particular task or project should take you (ask your supervising partner before you begin) and stick to the time frame allotted, says Beverly Bracker, Director of Career Services at Thomas Jefferson School of Law. Also understand and estimate how much time you will have left after finishing your work obligations—and be realistic about the amount of time you'll get to spend outside of work.

  If you're making the choice to work for an employer that requires a high time commitment every week, you should recognize that you won't have as much time left over to tend to the rest of your life, and you should set your schedule (both on and off the job) accordingly.

- Block out times when you can fully focus on things that need your full attention, Bracker suggests. Multitasking gets a lot of press and attention, but it isn't always possible—in some cases, you'll have to focus entirely on an important work project and cannot be distracted. You must quickly learn what types of tasks will need your undivided attention, recognize those tasks as they cross your desk, and block out sufficient time for them.

- Get rid of your major distractions—for example, e-mail and instant messages can take your attention away from tasks that need it, Bracker points out. Minimize (or if possible, cut out completely) the amount of time you spend on things that you find are repeatedly distracting you from your work.

- Use your support staff to help save you time. There are certain tasks you have to do yourself; others can be delegated to a capable person who works for you. Focus on the projects and assignments that you have to do on your own, and ask for help from support staff and others who can take over some of your projects.

- Use technology to your advantage. Learn about various methods of technology—from litigation software to electronic dockets—that can make your job easier. Ask for help from the experts, whether it's your firm's information technology person, an outside service provider, or a provider of technical continuing legal education who can help you pinpoint programs and technology that can help you save time in the long run.

- Develop a time management system that works for you—and use it! Whether it's daily reminders that pop up within Outlook, a diligently kept calendar, or a spreadsheet that tracks all of your deadlines and your progress on work projects and assignments, you have to have a system in place to help you manage your time. Once you have your system in place, stick to it and use it daily.

- Manage all of your commitments in one place. Time management is a challenge for young lawyers not just because of tight work schedules but also because new lawyers need to tend to work and their commitments outside of the firm, explains Paula Zimmer, Assistant Dean and Director of Career Services at Western New England School of Law. Whether it's family time or volunteer work, track every commitment you have in your calendar to help you manage your time.

Managing Your Money

If this is the first time you're making a regular paycheck, paying regular bills, and keeping track of your personal finances, chances are you may be lost in the numbers. You may be used to being on a budget, but as a new lawyer, you'll quickly have to master money management as well. In addition to managing your own money, as a new lawyer (and depending on your job and your employer), you may also be entrusted with client funds—all the more reason to learn the basics of sound financial management as early as possible.

The biggest challenge is not to let your lifestyle creep up on you, explains Jason Wu Trujillo, Senior Assistant Dean for Admissions and Financial Aid at the University of Virginia School of Law. When you first become a lawyer, you'll likely make more money than you made as a law student and before, which can bring with it the temptation to spend like there's no tomorrow.

But don't automatically skyrocket your bills and expenses by adopting the lifestyle of a lawyer, Trujillo says—rather, live like a student for a few more years so that you can keep your expenses down as much as possible while earning money. Doing so will give you a lot more freedom a few years down the line, Trujillo explains, when you may find yourself considering lifestyle changes or contemplating another job.

To help you manage your money, consider the following steps:

1. Figure out how much money you will make during each pay period.

2. Establish your budget: Write down every known bill that you'll have to pay, and estimate any expenses that are not constant, such as groceries.

3. Establish a system for tracking your income and expenses as soon as you are hired; this may be a simple spreadsheet or financial software that keeps track of your income and expenses.

4. Establish a system for paying bills—from getting checks or signing up for online bill pay to picking a day of the week to pay bills, have an organized system for tackling finances each week.

5. Keep close track of your spending. Stick to the system of money management that you have set up for yourself and keep an organized record of every dollar you earn, spend, and save.

THE ANSWERS—REVEALED!

Q: I'm about to enter the working world. How can I make sure I manage my finances well as a new lawyer?

A: First, establish a budget as soon as possible, says Dean Richard Matasar of New York Law School. Once you're hired, your employers can tell you how much you can expect to take home every pay period, Dean Matasar says. Figure out what your income is going to be and then figure out what your monthly bills are; then, reconcile your income and your expenses to be sure you aren't spending more than you earn.

Most importantly, stick to your budget and live within your means. Trim your expenses wherever you can, says Matasar: Live at home or with roommates, bag your lunches, don't misuse credit cards, and buy only things that you can afford.

Also seek help: Take advantage of resources your employer or your law school may offer you. Some employers offer financial management tools and formal or informal programs. Many law schools also offer exit counseling where a financial counselor can help you assess your debt load and provide you with information and resources for managing your finances. Some law schools also provide formal financial management programs and tips, such as Suffolk University Law School's Get $mart program.

Originally published in The National Jurist, *March 2009 issue*

Technology Resources

In today's fast-paced world, your understanding of and familiarity with technology can make or break you. You can learn
to use technology more effectively and increase your efficiency
and productivity as a new lawyer in the process. Start with
the following resources, recommended by the American Bar
Association's Legal Technology Resource Center. You can
find more resources listed on the LTRC's Web site,
www.abanet.org/tech/ltrc/.

Web Resources

- American Bar Association's Legal Technology Resource
  Center: Articles, reviews, presentations, surveys, compar-
  ison charts, annotated bibliographies, "how-to" guides,
  and more covering everything regarding the relationship
  between the practice of law and the use of technology.
  www.lawtechnology.org/

- ABA Site-tation: This blog from the ABA Legal
  Technology Resource Center highlights new or useful Web sites of interest to attorneys and other legal
  professionals and also alerts readers to new content on
  the ABA Legal Technology Resource Center Web site,
  as well as posting important news about technology
  that affects lawyers. Subscribe to the RSS feed or get a
  monthly e-mail compilation of new posts. http://
  new.abanet.org/sitetation/Pages/home.aspx

- ABA Journal Blawg Directory—Legal Technology
  Blogs: This section of the ABA Journal blog directory
  links to a variety of blogs by lawyers ("blawgs") dedicated to legal technology. Use the advanced search feature
  to do an aggregated search through thousands of blog
  postings. www.abajournal.com/blawgs/legal+technology

Periodicals

- GPSolo: Published eight times a year by the American Bar Association's General Practice, Solo and Small Firm Section, this magazine dedicates the June and December issues to technology. Current issue and archives available online. Print subscriptions are free to section members and cost $48 per year for nonmembers. www.abanet.org/genpractice/magazine/index.html

- Technology eReport: Published quarterly by the American Bar Association's General Practice, Solo and Small Firm Section, the eReport is delivered automatically via e-mail to GP Solo Division members, and back issues are archived online. www.abanet.org/genpractice/ereport/

- Law Practice Magazine: Published eight times a year by the American Bar Association's Law Practice Management Section. Current issue and archives are available online. Print subscriptions are free to section members and cost $68 per year for nonmembers. www.abanet.org/lpm/magazine/home.shtml

- Law Practice Today: Published monthly by the ABA's Law Practice Management Section. Published and archived online only. Subscriptions are free and available via RSS or through e-mail. www.abanet.org/lpm/lpt/

E-mail Discussion Lists and Web Forums

- ABA LawTech: An unmoderated e-mail discussion list dedicated to technology usage and issues in the practice of law hosted by the ABA Legal Technology Resource

Center. Searchable archives are available to anyone. http://mail.abanet.org/archives/lawtech.html

- Solosez: An unmoderated e-mail discussion list open to any topic, but often focused on technology in the small/solo firm practice setting. Searchable archives are available for subscribers. Hosted by the ABA GPSolo Division, this list is extremely busy. www.abanet.org/soloseznet/index.html

- ABA Law Practice Management Forums: These unmoderated (but monitored) Web forums focus on law practice management issues, including technology. Sponsored by the ABA Law Practice Management Section and available only to ABA members. www.abanet.org/lpm/forums.shtml

Conferences

- ABA TECHSHOW: This annual technology conference is held in Chicago in March/April and is sponsored by the American Bar Association's Law Practice Management Section. ABA TECHSHOW 2008 saw more than 2,000 attendees, 120 vendors, and 60+ legal technologists presenting more than 50 educational sessions. www.techshow.com/

Summation

- Hone your organizational skills for maximum efficiency.

- Set up regimented and clear systems for your workspace, your files, your wardrobe, your carrying bag, your databases, and your computer in order to become more organized at work and therefore be more efficient and productive.

- Practice diligent time management skills to ensure that you are meeting your deadlines and spending your time wisely on your tasks and projects.

- Learn to budget and manage your money as soon as you start working and practice sound money management skills.

Homework

- Track your schedule closely for one month. Write down as precisely as possible (to the minute, if you can manage) what you spend your time on, whether it's a work assignment or working out. At the end of the month, you'll be able to go over your personal "timesheets" and determine whether you're spending your time efficiently. Ask yourself these questions:

  - Are you spending too much time doing any particular tasks?

  - Are you sticking to the timeframes you've allotted for each task?

  - Are you spending too little time doing things that you enjoy (risking burnout and stress in the process)?

  - In what areas of time management might you improve?

- Track your income and your spending closely for one month. Write down as precisely as possible (to the penny, if you can manage) what you spend your money on, documenting your income and your spending. At the end of the month, assess whether your spending habits are in line with your goals for budgeting, saving, and spending your money. Ask yourself these questions:

- What sources of spending might you cut down on or cut out entirely?

- What are some of the sources of spending that you could potentially reduce—perhaps by organizing your life better and thinking ahead more before you spend?

- Are you sticking to your budget, or is there room for improvement?

- Are you saving enough money for your short-term and long-term plans?

CHAPTER 13

ETHICS, PROFESSIONALISM, WORKPLACE ETIQUETTE, AND INTERACTING WITH OTHERS

What are some of the dilemmas regarding ethics and professionalism that can affect young lawyers? This chapter details them and gives tips for avoiding unethical and unprofessional conduct; it also offers advice on office interactions with clients, supervisors, peers and colleagues, and others.

An Ethics Primer for Young Lawyers

There's no surefire way to get a job as a new lawyer, but there is a surefire way to lose one: by failing to comport with the rules of ethics or rules of professional conduct that are prescribed to all attorneys. Ethics are codes of conduct or behavior by which members of a particular profession have to abide. Lawyers must comport with the ethics codes of their jurisdictions, many of which are based on the *Model Rules of Professional Conduct*.

As a new lawyer, you must familiarize yourself with the ethics rules that pertain to attorneys in your jurisdiction and ensure that you are comporting with them. In particular, there are a handful of potential mistakes young lawyers may make on the job. For example:

- Rule 5.2 of the *Model Rules of Professional Conduct* deals specifically with the responsibilities of subordinate attorneys. The rule makes it clear that a lawyer is bound by the *Rules of Professional Conduct* notwithstanding that the lawyer acts at another person's direction. In fact, you should know that some courts have held subordinate lawyers responsible for simply "following orders" where the subordinate lawyer engaged in unethical conduct at the urging of his or her supervising attorney.

- Conversely, you must also understand the requirements imposed on supervisory lawyers and the repercussions of your own unethical conduct on your supervising lawyers as well. Rule 5.1 of the *Model Rules of Professional Conduct* calls for "reasonable efforts" by supervising lawyers to ensure that the firm has in place "measures giving reasonable assurance" that all lawyers conform to the *Rules of Professional Conduct*. Rule 5.1 also makes it clear that a lawyer with direct supervisory authority over another lawyer must employ reasonable efforts to ensure that the subordinate lawyer complies with the *Rules*.

- As a new lawyer, you'll be handling confidential and privileged files and cases. As such, you must make sure that you are familiar with your jurisdiction's professional rules regarding client confidentiality (which can be found in Rule 1.6 of the *Model Rules*) and evidentiary rules regarding the attorney-client privilege and the work-product privilege.

- Conflicts of interest present another area of potential conflict and liability. As a new lawyer, you must understand what constitutes a potential conflict of interest, what conflicts you must avoid, what conflicts may be imputed to the rest of your firm, and what the repercussions are for having a conflict.

Tips for Avoiding Unprofessional Conduct

Acting unethically can land you in some serious hot water, but acting unprofessional (even when you stay within the bounds of legal ethics) can also reflect badly upon you, may cause you to lose your partners and associates' respect, and in some cases may even cost you your job. Here are some common pitfalls and ways to avoid them.

- Not presenting yourself as a professional, polished, and courteous attorney. (See Chapter 5 for additional tips.)

- Neglecting your job obligations. Not only will this make your employer think twice about your value to the firm, but you must also remember that the rules of professional responsibility impose professional competence on attorneys. When you neglect your job obligations and fail to competently serve your clients, you are opening yourself up to liability under the ethics rules—which can range from steep fines to suspension of your law license to even disbarment.

- Being untruthful or untrustworthy. Again, in addition to the negative light in which this places you with your employer, lying or cheating may also subject you to liability under the ethics rules.

- Improperly interacting with clients, colleagues, supervisors, and others. (Read on for specific tips and mistakes to avoid.)

REVEALED!

"A professional young lawyer is one who strives to serve clients to the best of his or her capacity while contributing to the pursuit of justice and the furtherance of the rule of law.... I maintain familiarity with the ethical rules of my state and seek further information if there is ever an ethical question that I cannot answer. I would encourage other young lawyers to maintain the highest level of integrity and professional ethical knowledge possible in order to preserve the honor of our profession."

Christie Edwards, asylum attorney and adjunct professor; 2007 Thomas Jefferson School of Law graduate

The Ten Commandments of Ethics and Professionalism for Young Lawyers

The following ten tips were originally published by the Center for Law Student Ethics and Professionalism at the Massachusetts School of Law, which I co-founded with Associate Dean Michael L. Coyne. Visit the Center's Web site at www.lawstudentethics.com for more information about young lawyer ethics and professionalism.

1. First, be familiar with what your jurisdiction's ethics rules require of you. You may have come a long way from your law school's ethics class and those many interesting ethical conundrums, but knowing the requirements of legal ethics in the jurisdiction in which you're practicing is essential—you can't comport your conduct with the rules if you aren't familiar with them.

2. Ask for help, training, and guidance whenever you need it, and seek it out from whomever will give it. One of the biggest mistakes you could make as a young lawyer—one that can result in negligent, unprofessional or unethical conduct—stems from performing a task that you don't have the knowledge or competence to do. Learn to recognize when you need help and seek that help freely from someone more experienced or knowledgeable.

3. Align yourself with some great mentors on and off the job. Even if your firm doesn't have formal mentoring, you should seek out informal mentors who can guide you. In addition, many state, local, and specialty bar associations offer formal mentoring programs.

4. Polish your professional image. This includes the way you dress, speak, write, and generally present yourself—whether it's in person, online, or in correspondence. Think about the image you'd like to project to clients, employers, and others and keep that image in mind as you conduct yourself.

5. Continue your education and professional development. Law school may have taught you to think like a lawyer, but chances are, your real training in the practice of law begins when you start to practice. Seek out continuing legal education opportunities, seminars, or Web-based learning to help you hone your skills and continue learning about your chosen practice area.

6. Continue building your network. Whether you're in your first job or your dream job, continuing to build professional relationships and meet new people in your field is important—networking will not only increase your chances of getting employment in the future, but will also keep you connected and up to date with the profession. Take every chance to meet lawyers, whether by joining professional organizations, getting involved with your local young lawyers' associations, or attending professional and social events.

7. Be mindful of your conduct, both at work and outside of the firm. Avoid unprofessional, unethical, and especially criminal conduct at all times, and don't associate with people who engage in any of that: Remember that such conduct, even when it's after hours, can still get you in trouble with your state's bar overseers or enforcers.

8. Be wary of burnout. Despite many firms' efforts to provide better flexibility, it's no secret that many lawyers work long hours and struggle to find work-life balance. Lawyers are also more susceptible to substance abuse, depression, and stress than people in most other professions, according to a recent study.

   Learn to recognize the signs of burnout in yourself and cope with stress in healthy ways. Seek help for substance abuse and mental health issues immediately; many state bars and related organizations offer confidential help specifically for lawyers.

9. Don't take shortcuts on the job. Do the work right the first time to avoid wasting time—not to mention looking unprofessional or lazy in front of your employers or clients. Hone your time management skills: Learn to compartmentalize various tasks, prioritize, and plan ahead.

10. Look for a career path that's the right fit. Assess your career goals, strengths, and weaknesses and figure out what you'd like to do. Remember that few people start out in their dream jobs, and keep the big picture in mind when making career decisions.

"Right fit" is an often overused and misunderstood expression. To me, it means getting paid reasonably well to do a job you love to do that provides enough downtime to enjoy your life outside the law. Most people live to work, not work to live, so find what's right for you.

If the 100-hour-a-week job that pays outrageous money and has you traveling the country litigating cases makes you happy, then go for it. If you prefer the 40-hour-a-week associate's position that pays you well and also leaves time to coach your daughter's soccer team some afternoons, then you should find that job. The bottom line is that you're making a serious decision about what to do with the rest of your life. Take some time to set your priorities, establish your goals, and figure out the right path for you.

REVEALED!

"Handle clients and opposing counsel with respect. And, at the same time, stand your ground and keep your composure when experienced (opposing) counsel attempt to push the envelope.... Always consult with more senior and more trusted practitioners when your antennae warn you that there are ethical considerations lurking around the corner."

Amir Atashi Rang, principal at The Atashi Rang Law Firm and a 2000 UC Hastings graduate

Paying Attention to Diversity

For many new lawyers, working for a diverse employer—or an employer that simply appreciates and addresses the concerns of diverse employees—is vital. But employer diversity should be important to every new lawyer. Read on to find out why and to find out what you should look for in an employer in terms of diversity and cultural sensitivity.

THE ANSWERS—REVEALED!

Q: I hear a lot about diversity at law firms—why should I care about this issue?

A: Over the years, diversity at law firms has become a key component of law firm management, says Jack Yeh, partner in the litigation department at Manatt Phelps & Phillips, LLP, and co-chair of the firm's diversity program. Diversity doesn't just mean adequate representation of ethnicities; it is an all-encompassing cultural issue that includes gender, sexual orientation, socioeconomic status, and life experiences in general.

Everyone should be concerned with diversity efforts, says Yeh, as a diverse work environment also means a vibrant and challenging workplace. Diversity brings more opportunities to learn from each other and more opportunities to explore other viewpoints, philosophies, and ways of thinking. That's a big part of what makes college and law school fun, Yeh points out, and it's no different in the workplace. There's also a business case for diversity, Yeh says: A firm's best resource is its people, and clients—particularly businesses—increasingly expect firms to include diverse attorneys.

Besides, a firm's commitment to diversity or lack thereof is a great indicator of its commitment to its associates in general, from providing an inclusive workplace that's conducive to growth and professional development to offering work-life balance, says Elaine Arabatzis, Diversity/Pro Bono Counsel at Dickstein Shapiro, LLC. In fact, Arabatzis says many "majority" applicants that she interviews ask about the firm's commitment to diversity because they recognize that diversity means an environment in which they can grow and evolve professionally.

Q: What should I look for in the diversity efforts of the law firms where I interview?

A: Go beyond the brochures, says Yeh. Simply stating that the firm is an "equal opportunity employer" no longer cuts it; rather, you should be looking for firms that are inclusive and proudly sport an interesting array of associates and partners. Don't just look at the number of minorities or women employed by the firm. Look at indicators of their inclusion and success, such as the length of time people have been at the firm and their enthusiasm for the job they do, Yeh says.

Pay attention behind the scenes, Arabatzis recommends. When you're being led to and from your interview, for instance, pay attention to how people at the firm interact with each other. Is there a team-oriented, collegial atmosphere that includes every employee, from partners to associates to legal staff? Don't be afraid to ask direct questions, even if they are difficult ones, says Arabatzis; doing so will paint you as a candidate who's not afraid to look beyond the surface and advocate for yourself, which is the kind of lawyer-like behavior interviewers look for.

(continued)

(continued)

Research the firm's general reputation for diversity and work-life balance as well. Associate satisfaction surveys are particularly good indicators of the "real deal" behind a firm's diversity efforts, Arabatzis says, as they are usually anonymous and depict the opinions of associates who were in your shoes just a couple of years ago. Blogs can be another great source for insider info.

Also look for mentoring opportunities and other programs to assist new associates—both general programs and those specifically geared towards minorities, women, and other groups, Yeh says. If the firm has successful mentors and role models from all walks of life, that indicates opportunities for success all around.

Originally published in The National Jurist, *November 2007 issue*

Etiquette Tips on the Job

Workplace etiquette is important, even more so for lawyers than many others because the law is a people profession that requires lawyers to interact with many different people daily. In fact (and perhaps not surprisingly), Americans expect a higher degree of professionalism from lawyers and doctors than others, says Mandie Araujo, Director of Career Services at New England Law|Boston, who has founded a company called Pardon Me, which helps legal professionals with workplace etiquette issues.

Consider the following workplace etiquette tips:

- Understand that there are workplace etiquette hierarchies in place: The client is at the top, Araujo details. Then come the managing and the senior partners, followed by junior partners and then associates. As a new lawyer, law clerk, or summer associate, you are at the very bottom, Araujo says, so make sure that you show respect and deference to everyone.

- Engage in positive conversation and use positive body language. Avoid inappropriate or informal language in the office, recommends Paula Zimmer, Assistant Dean and Director of Career Services at Western New England School of Law, and also stay out of office gossip.

- Don't ask people for a job right after you meet them, Araujo stresses. Instead, work to develop a human and professional bond with the person first, and then ask whether you may forward them your resume or tell them about yourself, disclosing that you're looking for a position.

- Familiarize yourself with any formal policies and procedures that your firm has in place on issues dealing with professionalism and etiquette. For example, the firm may have a specific dress code, clear rules on breaks and hours worked, and even particular rules on office relationships. Be sure you know what those rules are, and be sure you adhere to them.

- Also take stock of the firm's etiquette concerns informally. Part of exhibiting good workplace etiquette skills is knowing how to act around your colleagues and being able to fit into your workplace. Take a look around to see how more senior lawyers at your firm behave; for example:

  - How do they dress?

  - When and for how long do they take lunch and breaks?

- What seem to be the accepted mores and customs at the firm?

- When you attend networking events, and even when you go to work every single day, make sure you realize how far-reaching your contacts really are. Don't take advantage of your relationships with lawyers, Araujo says. Recognize that workplace etiquette and successful professional relationships go hand in hand and that you need to contribute to those relationships as opposed to just taking from them.

Tips for Interacting with Clients

- Get to know who your clients are and what your clients want, says Ari Kaplan. This means knowing not only your clients' names and personal information, but also your clients' goals and the ways that your work can fit into meeting those goals. For example, if you're working at a firm with corporate clients and their in-house law departments, then you should understand the internal make-up of the law department, the environment in which corporate counsel work, the roles of corporate counsel, and your role as outside counsel.

- Understand that your clients are at the "top of the food chain" and accordingly offer them the utmost respect, courtesy, professionalism, and deference.

- With clients—perhaps even more so than others—aim to develop a formal (professional) relationship and be careful not to slip into a bond that becomes too informal for the precarious attorney-client relationship.

- Be mindful of all of the rules of ethics and professional responsibility that govern your conduct as an attorney in your jurisdiction, particularly those that specifically govern the attorney-client relationship.

  For example, you should be keenly aware of the rules covering confidential client communications and information; conflicts of interest; the inception, scope, and termination of the attorney-client relationship; the rules on communicating with clients; and the rules regarding your role as advocate, advisor, and counselor.

Tips for Interacting with Partners and Superiors

- Put simply, get to know the "stories" behind your supervising attorneys and partners, recommends Kaplan. In general, Kaplan says it's essential to learn as much as you can about those people with whom you would like to interact, whether they are peers or superiors: When you understand the background of someone you are trying to meet, he adds, you can easily find a way to highlight what he or she is doing as an opportunity to better get to know the person.

  Study the background of a supervisor—if you see that he or she is doing something interesting, interview them, says Kaplan (as if you were, say, interviewing them for a profile in a local paper or trade publication). Use the interview as an opportunity to develop an initial connection, says Kaplan.

- Develop a good dose of humility, says Trisha Fillbach, Director of Career Development at Drake Law School.

While the vast majority of new graduates are eager to learn and understand that they need training, on the other end of the spectrum are those few who believe they already know everything, Fillbach explains. While this overconfidence can be appropriate in certain situations, a new associate must figure out when to use it and how to express it in the most effective manner.

- Conversely, do take pride in your work and don't let any insecurities control your actions. When you're dealing with supervisors, you need to exude confidence (just as you would when you're dealing with a client) and be proud of the work product you've churned out that you know is good.

- On that note, do make sure your work product is thorough and impressive. Don't forget that you will get your work from partners or senior associates. How well you satisfy these supervisors with your work product will determine how much work you will get from them in the future and, in turn, determine your value to the employer, says Fillbach.

- Learn how to "manage up," recommends Zimmer. There's a fine art to being able to manage a boss, she adds: You have to learn to do this effectively but at the same time do it gently and respectfully—such as by suggesting changes rather than forcing them, by sitting down with your boss in private to offer suggestions, and by using mild guidance rather than forceful fits.

- Find supervising attorneys and partners at your firm whom you look up to and would like to emulate, says Jason Wu Trujillo, Senior Assistant Dean for Admissions and Financial Aid at the University of Virginia School of Law. Whether it's emulating the partner's style of conducting trials, wanting to adopt some of the partner's best practices in business development, or simply admiring the way the partner balances work with other obligations, have some role models in place—at your firm and elsewhere, if possible—whom you can look up to.

REVEALED!

"It's important to engage your superiors by staying in front of them and asking good questions. These outcomes will be beneficial when it's time to promote an associate. By communicating with your superiors, it demonstrates to them you care about your job as well as your career.... It is important to be able to separate business from personal. Criticism could be constructive. Most first-year associates have a hard time separating a superior's criticism from what he or she thinks of you personally."

Nikon Limberis, equity trader and 2007 New York Law School graduate

Interacting with Your Peers and Other Associates

Practicing civility is essential—even when you're met with something less than civil behavior! Some new graduates are taken aback by the lack of civility exhibited by some lawyers, says Fillbach.

While in law school, students are taught about the importance of civility and working in collaboration. Working together in a more benign setting like law school, most students find this to be the norm; however, once out in the practice, some graduates find a different type of opposing counsel: one that is more aggressive and less collaborative, Fillbach explains. While most new lawyers will easily acclimate to different attorney styles and discern between the least and most desirable, an ultra-sensitive attorney can find it a bit more challenging.

The first step, of course, is to acclimate yourself to a potentially more stressful and challenging environment—but, more importantly, to practice civility in the face of peers who don't, Fillbach stresses. Remember that there will always be opposing counsel, co-counsel, or even attorneys whom you work with daily at your own firm who act unethically or unprofessionally, but your job is to ensure that you remain civil to them even when they do.

New lawyers should also remember to use relationships with peers and colleagues to their advantage, experts say. Your peers, classmates, and colleagues are a great source for networking and even business development: They may help you when you need a resource, serve as a sounding board when you need advice or just need to talk about the frustrations of being a new lawyer, and refer clients to you when they need your expertise. Remember the golden rule when it comes to interacting with your peers and colleagues!

Summation

- Understand what the rules of professional responsibility in your jurisdiction require of you and be sure that you comport with those rules at all times.

- Avoid some of the common ethical and professional mistakes that young lawyers make.

- Recognize that your clients are the lifeblood of your business and treat them with the utmost respect and deference.

- Interact with your supervisors with respect as well and aim to develop valuable professional relationships with your partners and superiors.

- Maintain civility when interacting with clients, peers, colleagues, supervisors, and others, and remember the golden rule in all of your professional interactions.

Homework

- Make a list of five to ten people whom you know professionally but would like to get to know better in your professional career. What are some questions you would like to ask each person? What intrigues you about each person as a professional?

- Think of one situation where you acted without the kind of professionalism or conduct that you're striving to project as a new lawyer and make notes about it. Next, pinpoint what specific mistakes you made or what you did wrong in that situation. Finally, make some notes about specific things that you would do to correct your mistake, as well as specific things you would do differently if you found yourself in the same situation again.

CHAPTER 14

MAINTAINING WORK-LIFE BALANCE, PREVENTING BURNOUT, AND MANAGING YOUR STRESS LEVEL

This chapter details key issues that affect young lawyers, including diversity, work-life balance, pro bono work, preventing burnout, and maintaining your sanity in a stressful profession.

Maintaining Work-Life Balance

Your first year as a new attorney may be the most difficult in terms of balancing because you are gauging expectations and you want to impress, so you seek out a large workload, explains Trisha Fillbach, Director of Career Development at Drake Law School. For some people, this struggle never goes away, Fillbach concedes, but she adds that it's critical for young lawyers to maintain some sort of balance to prevent burnout. Work-life balance is one of those issues in the legal field that has gotten plenty of attention and press in recent years, and many new lawyers and graduating law students seem to have the goal of maintaining some semblance of a balanced schedule at the top of their lists.

Of course, if you just graduated law school, you are probably used to having a grueling workload, having little time for yourself, and scarcely having true balance in your life. Still, while being a student may have meant doing lots of work and studying, it doesn't compare to the 80-hour work weeks you'll likely find as a new lawyer, along with having to tend to numerous outside obligations—not the least of them paying your own bills and being responsible for managing your own finances for what may be the first time.

Consider the following tips for maintaining work-life balance:

- Understand that the concept of balance is imperfect: Perfect balance is virtually unattainable, and you should simply aim to have some semblance of balance that keeps you happy on and off the job. On any given day, your balance may go off-kilter, explains Ellen Ostrow, Ph.D., Founder of Lawyers' Life Coach, Inc., who counsels legal professionals on maintaining balance, so you must learn to measure work-life balance in longer increments (weeks or months) rather than mere hours or days.

- Make time for yourself. A feeling of balance is imbedded in your own internal experience, Ostrow explains. You have to figure out what matters to you and make time for it, whether it's Sunday dinner with your family or regular exercise. Figure out what activities are important to you and set aside time for them.

- Set realistic goals for yourself, both at work and outside of it. When you're new to the practice of law, you must understand and recognize that balance can be very elusive: You are expected to work long hours and work harder than you ever have. That said, you must understand your own limits—both at work and outside—and stay within the boundaries you set for yourself; this means you have to learn to sometimes say no to projects, engagements, or invitations that come your way.

- Reach out to others. Having a support system in place such as a trusted mentor can help with achieving balance as well, says Fillbach. Talk with other new lawyers and young associates about how they manage to find balance in their lives, and ask trusted mentors and supervisors for their advice and insights.

Spotting the Signs of Burnout: A Self-Assessment Questionnaire

You may understand that you need to maintain a level of balance between your work and the rest of your life, but can you recognize the signs of first-year associate burnout? To determine whether you exhibit any warning signs, ask yourself the following questions:

- Are you experiencing any changes in sleep patterns?

- Are you experiencing any changes in your appetite?

- Are you abusing drugs, alcohol, prescription medications, caffeine, or other substances?

- Are you experiencing any health problems related to stress?

- Has your schedule changed drastically in the recent past?

- Has your workload substantially changed in the recent past?

- Have you stopped or drastically reduced doing activities outside of work which were sources of pleasure and balance for you in the past? (For example, have you stopped seeing family and friends, paying attention to your physical or mental health, or engaging in activities that you normally enjoy?

- Do you consistently dread going in to work or facing most of your work assignments?

- Do you feel like you're exhausted all or most of the time?

- Do you constantly feel like the work you do does not make a difference or is not appreciated?

- Do you find the majority of your work assignments to be majorly overwhelming—or, conversely, mind-numbing?

- Do you feel like you have little or no control over your work?

- Do you constantly try to "do it all" on and off the job?

If you've answered "yes" to many of these questions, you may be at risk for job-related burnout, which can lead to lack of balance and serious health issues. Get some help and consult some resources! On its Web site, www.pardc.org, the Project for Attorney Retention lists the following valuable online resources on attorney work-life balance:

- Ostrow, Ellen, and Naomi Beard, *Beyond the Billable Hour*, free e-mail newsletter about work/life balance for attorneys, www.lawyerslifecoach.com

- Center for Gender in Organizations, Simmons Graduate School of Management, http://www.simmons.edu/som/

- The Washington Work/Life Coalition, www.worklifecoalition.org

- Boston College Center for Work & Family, www.bc.edu/schools/csom/cwf/center/overview.html

- The National Partnership for Women and Families, www.nationalpartnership.org

- Cornell Employment and Family Careers Institute, www.blcc.cornell.edu

- The Center for Working Families, http://workingfamilies.berkeley.edu/

- Families and Work Institute, www.familiesandwork.org/

- Work-Family Researchers Electronic Network, sponsored by the Alfred P. Sloan Foundation, http://wfnetwork.bc.edu/

- Center for Work & Family, www.workfamily.com

- Montgomery Work/Life Alliance, www.worklifemontgomery.org

- Working Moms Refuge, www.momsrefuge.com

- Catalyst, www.catalystwomen.org/home.html

- The Glass Ceiling, www.theglassceiling.com

- Working Mother, www.workingmother.com

- Working Woman, www.workingwomanmag.com

- Radcliffe Public Policy Center, www.radcliffe.edu/
  pubpol/index.html

- The Kunz Center for the Study of Work & Family,
  Department of Sociology at the University of Cincinnati,
  http://ucaswww.mcm.uc.edu/sociology/kunzctr/

Performing Pro Bono Work

Many law students begin law school with the intention of
entering a public interest or social justice position upon graduation—or at least working a job that allows them to do some
work "pro bono": performing free or low-cost services for clients who can't afford legal representation.

Some states have mandated pro bono requirements, where
lawyers have to perform a set number of hours of work pro
bono every year. Other states don't mandate yearly pro bono
but strongly encourage lawyers to provide it; many employers
also require or encourage pro bono service from their associates.

If you're interested in getting involved in pro bono help, consider the following tips:

- Choose a project with personal meaning. Discern what
  causes matter to you and get involved in something that
  you will personally enjoy participating in. As a new lawyer, your time is limited and should be spent on things
  that matter to you.

- Budget your time carefully: Enter pro bono projects
  with a clear understanding of the time and effort they
  will require of you, and make sure you are allotting all of
  your projects—including volunteer work and community
  service—sufficient time to make them successful.

- Check with your employer about any pro bono initiatives that are already in place at the firm and get involved. If the firm doesn't engage in firm-wide or corporate pro bono initiatives, you can opt to start a new initiative and get your colleagues involved—just be sure that you consider the firm, the project, the potential clients, and any lawyers who will be involved when choosing and establishing a new initiative.

REVEALED!

"I take asylum cases occasionally if they fit with my teaching schedule and if it is for a client who truly needs my help. I make sure that I have the time to devote to the case while also making sure that I can fulfill my other personal and professional obligations. I would encourage other young attorneys to make sure they have a hobby or form of relaxation so they can be personally as well as professionally fulfilled."

Christie Edwards, asylum attorney and adjunct professor; 2007 Thomas Jefferson School of Law graduate

Managing Your Stress Level and Maintaining Your Sanity

It's no secret that the life of a lawyer is rife with stress. In fact, some experts say lawyers have some of the highest rates of job dissatisfaction, suicide, and substance abuse issues out of all professions and trades surveyed!

In addition to maintaining some semblance of work-life balance, it's essential that you stay away from some unhealthy and very dangerous habits that may result from the immense stress of becoming a new lawyer. If you're having trouble with substance abuse, stress, or depression, get help immediately. Consult the following resources:

- The American Bar Association's Commission on Lawyer Assistance Programs offers helpful information, resources, and referrals on its Web site at http://ww.abanet.org/legalservices/colap/.

- Your state's Lawyers Helping Lawyers or Lawyers Concerned for Lawyers organization can help you overcome issues with substance abuse, depression, and stress and provide you with support groups and information about managing your stress level and maintaining your sanity.

What Are Lawyer Assistance Programs?

Lawyer assistance programs provide free resources, counseling, education, and help for attorneys, judges, law students, and—in some jurisdictions—even family members. Most states have lawyer assistance programs in place; take advantage of them. Some lawyers mistakenly believe that lawyer assistance programs are only there to help with addiction and substance abuse issues, but that is not the case—they can also provide free, confidential, and valuable help with

- Managing stress

- Keeping burnout in check

- Work-life balance

- Relationship issues

- Career concerns

- Maintaining your sanity

Also, many lawyer assistance programs offer valuable help with practice management. Massachusetts and Washington, as just two examples, run comprehensive law office management assistance programs, which offer free professional assistance with office administration—a must for small firms and solo attorneys, but helpful for any lawyer who's new on the job.

In addition, according to the American Bar Association's Web site, "The Commission on Lawyer Assistance Programs (CoLAP)—a service entity of the ABA—educates the legal profession concerning alcoholism, chemical dependencies, stress, depression, and other emotional health issues and also assists and supports all bar associations and LAPs in developing and maintaining methods of providing effective solutions for recovery. For more information about the myriad of services provided by CoLAP, check out its Web site at www.abanet.org/legalservices/colap/ or call the CoLAP hotline at 866-LAW-LAPS (866-529-5277)."

Gina Walcott, Executive Director of Lawyers Concerned for Lawyers, Inc., in Massachusetts, recommends that new lawyers check out the following additional resources:

- American Institute of Stress, www.stress.org

- HelpGuide.Org on Stress, www.helpguide.org/mental

- Mind/Body Medical Institute, www.mbmi.org

- On-Site Academy, www.onsiteacademy.org

- The Project for Attorney Retention, www.pardc.org

- Bipolar/Depression Disorders Information Center, http://mentalhealth.samhsa.gov/publications/allpubs/ken98-0049/default.asp

- Families for Depression Awareness, www.familyaware.org

- Lawyers with Depression, www.lawyerswithdepression.com

- About Depression, http://depression.about.com

- Depression and Bipolar Support Alliance, http://www.dbsalliance.org/site/PageServer?pagename=home

- Depression and Related Affective Disorders Association (DRADA), www.drada.org/

- Child & Adolescent Bipolar Foundation, www.bpkids.org/site/PageServer

- National Alliance for the Mentally Ill (NAMI), www.nami.org/

- National Institute of Mental Health, www.nimh.nih.gov

- American Psychological Association, www.apa.org

- American Psychiatric Publishing, www.appi.org/

- Archives of the Journal of General Psychiatry (AMA), http://archpsyc.ama-assn.org/

- Mental Health Infosource, www.cmellc.com/

Tips for Dealing with Stress

On her blog, *The Issues of Life in Law* (http://lclma.blogspot.com/), Walcott writes that there are certain experiences dealing with stress that should be simply taken as givens—while she writes for laid-off attorneys, her points ring true for all attorneys, especially those who are navigating the legal landscape for the first time.

1. There will be some degree of worry and stress.

2. There will be some level of interest in knowing who is (and is not) going through a similar experience.

3. There will be some people in your life who—for whatever reason—feel the need to constantly update you on how much worse things are than you thought.

4. There will be a point in time, however brief, when you experience self-doubt, lowered self-esteem, or decreased self-confidence.

5. At some point, it will take more of an effort than usual to keep up your social and professional relationships and to continue in your professional extracurricular activities.

To cope with those given stresses, Walcott offers the following pieces of advice:

- Don't get stuck worrying so much that you fall victim to self-defeating actions.

- Steer clear of naysayers and "voices of doom."

- Don't focus on bleak, hopeless, downtrodden perspectives (including media reports)—instead, focus on opportunities that may be out there for you.

- Accept whatever situation is stressing you out, but don't be labeled by it.

Summation

- Build good work-life balance habits early—if you implement them as a law student, you will be more likely to keep them as a lawyer.

- Make time for friends and family.

- Make time for yourself and the activities you enjoy.

- Consider the importance of pro bono work as it applies to your schedule, your work, and your preferences.

- Be mindful of problems with substance abuse, stress, and depression.

- Don't fall victim to burnout: Seek help at the first sign of a problem.

Homework

- Write down five to ten things that you enjoy making time for. Look at your list carefully and pinpoint the most important things on your list—what are some of the things that you cannot live without, that you must make time for in order to consider your life balanced?

PART III

THINKING AHEAD

Chapter 15: Making Them Want to Keep You

Chapter 16: Planning for Your Next Job

Chapter 17: Helpful Online Resources for Young
Lawyers

MAKING THEM WANT TO KEEP YOU

You may have landed that perfect position, but when it comes to career planning, your job is just beginning. Now, your focus must be on performing well and presenting to your employer that you are a valuable employee—in other words, making your employer want to keep you in the long run!

Many different factors go into this: showing initiative and going beyond the call of duty, increasing your efficiency and profitability, learning and honing the basic skills you'll need to have on the job, maintaining a positive attitude, interacting with the rest of the team and representing your firm well, and presenting a professional image are some of the most important examples.

Want specific information about being a valuable employee and increasing your staying power at the firm? Consider the following twenty tips:

1. Show initiative. Ask to take on additional assignments; affirmatively ask for feedback; and generally show that you are interested in the work, mission, and business of the firm.

2. Support the team efforts, says Charles Volkert of Robert Half Legal. Partners begin to take notice of first-year associates who demonstrate from the beginning that they recognize the value of team efforts, says Volkert. Gear your work towards supporting the whole enterprise and show that you are a good fit for the firm because you work well with others.

3. Understand how your work and your role fit into the firm's mission as a whole, and appreciate the "big picture." Don't just complete that memo or research assignment that your supervisor gave you—find out how your assignment fits into the entire case and follow up after you complete the assignment to show your employer that you're genuinely interested in your work at the firm.

4. Go above and beyond the typical "first-year call of duty." It's presumed that you will have great research and writing skills, or that you'll turn in good work product, so the way to stand out in the eyes of partners and other decision-makers is to do things that are not necessarily expected of you—such as asking for additional assignments, representing the firm in the community, and doing things without necessarily being asked.

5. Be flexible, Volkert stresses. During your first year on the job, you are bound to encounter internal processes and ways of doing things that are unfamiliar to you, Volkert explains. Even if you don't necessarily agree with those internal processes (or think you could do things better), resist the urge to constantly tell your employer about how things were done at your former job—or worse yet, in law school!

   Show flexibility and adapt to the ways that your current employer wants you to handle certain projects or do certain things. Part of being flexible, of course, is tackling whatever assignment comes your way—and doing it with a positive, enthusiastic attitude.

6. Observe the corporate culture, says Volkert. Assess and get accustomed to the firm's culture: Observe how attorneys interact with each other and then make a concerted effort to fit into the firm as a whole, Volkert says.

7. Learn to communicate effectively. You may have heard this in law school: A lawyer's bread and butter is his or her communication skills. You must hone your written and oral communication skills as a new lawyer; practically speaking, you must also learn the different communication styles that may work for different people.

   As an example, one partner may be delighted to share periodic formal feedback with you, while another may adopt more of a "no news is good news" outlook when it comes to feedback—you must be able to understand, gauge, and adapt to those different communication styles.

8. Treat everyone at the firm with respect, Volkert says. He adds that one common mistake young lawyers make is not showing deference to other associates or support staff. Don't think that you only need to be respectful towards partners and supervising attorneys: Associates, legal staff, and others may be keeping tabs on your work, progress, and behavior, and their insights may be considered when you're being evaluated on your performance and progress.

   Plus, Volkert points out that many support staff and other associates can provide you with invaluable insight—a paralegal can teach you some tricks of the trade when it comes to working on projects, and a more experienced associate can tell you about various partners' preferences when it comes to work product or working together.

9. Learn the "basics" quickly, Volkert says: whether it's filling out paperwork, learning the ins and outs of the computer system, or mastering the phones and the files, it's important to get the basics of the job quickly mastered so that you can better focus on honing your practical skills and increasing your substantive knowledge.

   Getting the basics of your job down pat will help you work more efficiently and increase your productivity. The further behind you fall on those basics, the more questions you'll be left with as you begin working at the firm, so take care of the basics early on.

10. Interact with your supervisors, peers, opposing counsel, clients, and others properly, professionally, and courteously. Remember that you must work to build your network as soon as you are hired (and preferably even before).

    Keep in mind that networking is a two-way street: It means building, cultivating, and maintaining professional relationships, which all requires a certain level of give and take from both parties.

    Aim to develop relationships that are based on respect and mutual professional conduct with your supervisors, peers, clients, and others—and avoid any interactions that may paint you as an unprofessional, unethical, or impolite lawyer.

11. Begin to hone your marketable skills and develop your book of business as soon as you are hired. In order to make yourself more valuable to your current employer and more marketable to prospective employers and clients, you must begin building your client base during the first year on the job and continue to hone your marketable skills.

12. Learn to manage your time well and aim for productivity and efficiency. Hone your organizational skills, keep meticulous track of your time, and avoid common productivity pitfalls such as failing to allocate your time wisely or not doing things right the first time.

13. Learn to ask for feedback and take constructive criticism well. Request formal evaluations and conduct periodic self-evaluations, assessing your strengths and weaknesses, your progress, and your goals. When you receive feedback, appreciate it (even if it's negative) and learn from it.

14. Learn from your mentors and others. During your first year on the job, you should aim to develop lasting mentoring relationships. Remember that you can find mentors in many places—from the senior partner who can help you with assignments to the senior associate who can fill you in on organizational culture. Seek guidance from many potential mentors and learn from others both on and off the job.

15. Maintain a positive attitude. Show energy and enthusiasm on the job, maintain a friendly and courteous demeanor, and strive to project to your employers that you are a part of the team.

16. Make the firm your main focus. Don't just concentrate on how a particular project or assignment or new initiative will benefit you; instead, show your employers how your involvement will benefit the firm and add value.

17. Project a professional image. Whether it's in person, in writing, or online, you should aim to present yourself as a mature, confident, knowledgeable, polite, and efficient individual. Being professional encompasses many different considerations, from the way you dress to the

way you speak, from the way you work to the way you behave on and off the job. Act accordingly.

18. This goes without saying: At all times, comport with the rules of ethics and professional responsibility that govern the conduct of attorneys in your jurisdiction.

19. Represent the firm well—to clients, potential clients, opposing counsel, and the general community. For starters, be knowledgeable and enthusiastic about the firm's business and understand what sets your employer apart from other firms. Present yourself as a polished professional and remember that you are the firm's ambassador to clients and others.

20. Beware of burnout. The first year on the job as a new lawyer comes with plenty of stress and internal and external pressures. Be sure you find a healthy outlet for managing those pressures, maintain some balance between your work and the rest of your life, and avoid unhealthy habits such as substance abuse and gambling.

REVEALED!

"Demeanor, work ethic, and being humble [all go into professionalism during the first year]. You need to know that you don't know anything and the older, more experienced attorneys know all (even if it's not true)!"

Greg Benoit, Worcester County Assistant District Attorney and 2007 Massachusetts School of Law graduate

Summation

- Show initiative and go beyond the call of duty.

- Increase your efficiency, productivity, and profitability to the firm.

- Learn and hone the basic skills you'll need to have on the job.

- Maintain a positive attitude.

- Interact with the rest of the team and represent your firm well.

- Present a professional image.

Homework

- Pick a colleague, peer, or supervisor at work whom you admire. Make a list of ten to twenty traits or skills that person possesses that you think make him or her stand out and succeed on the job.

CHAPTER 16

PLANNING FOR YOUR NEXT JOB

Your first job probably won't be your last—in fact, the National Association for Law Placement reports that 8.4 percent of entry-level associates leave their first jobs within 16 months of employment, and nearly one in five lateral hires departs from their employer within the first two years of being hired.

It's normal to move around and work for various employers—but if you plan on doing so, you'll want to make sure that your performance at your first position correlates to your plans for your next one!

Onward and Upward to Your Second Job

Here are 15 tips to prepare and plan for your second job as a lawyer:

1. Polish your networking skills. Remember that most positions come through networking efforts, not formal job applications.

2. Keep a detailed career journal of your assignments, your strengths and weaknesses, and your performance and progress on the job as a first-year associate.

3. Evaluate your own strengths and weaknesses; periodically re-evaluate your progress, your career plans, and your goals; and continue honing your skill set.

4. Engage in continuing legal education and professional development activities—doing so will not only help you hone your skill set but also expose you to tremendous networking opportunities.

5. Get involved in the legal community and in your community in general. Make connections, get to know people, get your name out there, and get noticed in a positive way.

6. Back up your skills with numbers—business development numbers, that is. With a solid book of business, you can go virtually anywhere, so work to develop great relations with your clients and bring in business to your current firm, which will help you market your business to other firms and employers down the line.

7. Become an expert at something. Offer your current and potential employer added value, whether it's mastering a particular e-discovery task or carving out a niche for yourself within your substantive focus.

8. Market your expertise. Write articles; answer legal questions online; share tips with your network; and overall make sure your employers, clients, and potential employers know how much you know and what you can do.

9. Keep informed about the legal landscape and potential employment opportunities in your local legal environment.

10. Keep informed about legal trends: Stay up-to-date about what's going on in your practice area, your local legal environment, and the legal landscape in general, and understand what potential employers are looking for in candidates.

11. Keep an open mind about potential employers. Don't discount alternative legal employers and even non-legal employers who may be interested in a JD with some experience in law practice.

12. Develop strategic partnerships with people who can help you find a job, from career coaches and counselors to legal recruiters.

13. Be proactive about finding your next job. Tell your network what you're looking for, affirmatively get your name out there, and don't rely on chance to have your dream job fall into your lap.

14. Show enthusiasm and energy about potential new positions. Remember that employers are not just looking for the right qualifications in employees, but also the right fit.

15. Focus on the potential employer—not just on yourself. Make sure it comes across to the employer that you will bring value to the firm, and show the potential employer how you could help them meet their needs and further their mission.

REVEALED!

"It is important to understand that your first job doesn't necessarily have to be the perfect fit. It could and should be viewed as a place to learn personally and professionally. If it ends up being someplace you spend a good part of your career, then that's gravy."

Nikon Limberis, equity trader and 2007 New York Law School graduate

Eight Proactive Steps Toward Changing Your Career Path

At some point, you may want to change your career path, or you may face a career change through some event in your work or your life. Transitions can be tough to navigate, but having a concrete plan for them may help. Consider taking the following eight steps toward a successful career change:

1. Pinpoint the reasons why you're seeking a change.

   - Are you looking to practice in a different area or looking for substantive projects that will keep you engaged and interested?

   - Are you looking for a different schedule or more flexibility?

   - Do you want a different kind of work environment?

   - Are you looking for a change because of life changes that you're going through?

   - Are you interested in leaving law practice?

   - Are you changing careers because of increased opportunities in your new field?

Before you can successfully change careers, you must assess and understand your reasons for wanting the change, and you have to do a certain level of self-assessment just as you did when you were thinking of your first job.

2. Pinpoint your needs. Career changes often happen because of a lifestyle change that has caused you to need or want to work in a different setting or environment. Write down what practical considerations and factors are influencing your decision, and also write down your "must-haves" in a potential new position.

3. Pinpoint your preferences. In addition to thinking about practical concerns, also think about what you'd like to get out of your career change and what you're personally looking for in your new position—from your interests to your long-term career plans and goals.

4. Pinpoint any past and current experiences that may help you make the transition. So many of the skills you develop in the first year on the job are transferable, says Paula Zimmer, Assistant Dean and Director of Career Services at Western New England School of Law. Capitalize on the parts of your first year that overlapped or are most transferable to the position that you're seeking. For example, if you're looking to transition into a public interest position serving low-income clients after working in private practice, then focus on the skills you developed as part of your pro bono work assisting low-income clients in the past. If you're looking to transition into a different practice area, focus on any tasks that you worked on in the past that overlapped and delved into that practice area.

5. Pinpoint the skills that you need to hone or acquire in order to make the transition, and figure out how you'll go about doing so. For example, are there substantive legal courses you could take that will help you develop a knowledge base that you need to have to make the transition?

6. Pinpoint the people who can help you with your transition.

   • Who do you know in the field that you want to enter?

   • Who may be able to assist you with getting a job in the field?

   • Who can tell you more about working in the field?

   • Who in your network may know others who can help you transition into the new field?

7. Pinpoint the steps you need to take toward your transition. Write down a clear-cut and comprehensive plan for making a change, including deadlines for various points in the transition and ideas for getting started.

8. Put your plan into action.

THE ANSWERS—REVEALED!

Q: Help: I'm about to graduate and have no job lined up! What should my next steps be?

A: In some years, the market for new associates can be tough, and things may look bleak if you're unfortunate enough not to have a job at graduation. Here are some final parting tips to get you started.

Come up with a concrete job search plan and put everything in writing. Assess your strengths, interests, and career

---

goals; pinpoint potential employers; and come up with a schedule for your job search, detailing how much time you'll spend accomplishing related tasks, such as attending networking events or sending out resumes. Then hold yourself to your plan.

If you haven't already done so, contact your law school's career services office ASAP. Present your job search plan to a career counselor and talk with the counselor about your options; your resume, cover letter, and writing samples; and leads and recommendations.

Stay flexible. Keep an open mind about potential job opportunities—you may have to reconsider your first preferences and consider various new options. Don't be afraid to take a job that isn't everything you've ever wanted, and use every job as an opportunity to learn, grow, and mold your career.

If you can afford it, consider applying for an unpaid position in your area of interest to gain experience while you continue searching for paid positions.

Network: Go out and meet lawyers, attend seminars and social functions, and build professional relationships.

Be proactive about your job search. Stay informed about the field and about employment opportunities, and don't wait for a job offer to find you.

Originally published in The National Jurist, *March 2009 issue*

Summation

- Remember that your first job likely won't be your last: keep in mind your career plans for your second job and beyond.

- Develop and market expertise in a particular skill or set of skills.

- Stay informed about the legal landscape, legal trends, and the outlook on the legal profession.

- Build your network.

- If you're interested in a career change, remember to plan and pinpoint each step you need to take to make that change, and then be proactive about putting your plans into action.

Homework

- Make a list of the five most challenging aspects of a potential career change, and then make an accompanying list of the practical steps you would take to handle and overcome each of those challenges.

- Make a list of the five most rewarding aspects of a potential career change. What would be your top reasons for changing career paths? How might your list change over time, or in light of various life changes?

CHAPTER 17

Helpful Online Resources for Young Lawyers

Need more information about your first year on the job as a new lawyer? Consider the following online resources.

Job Searching

- ABA Career Counsel, www.abanet.org/careercounsel/finding.html
- Craigslist, www.craigslist.org
- LawCrossing.com, www.lawcrossing.com
- Lawyers' Weekly Jobs, www.lawyersweeklyjobs.com
- Martindale-Hubbell, www.martindale.com
- Monster.com, www.monster.com
- Robert Half Legal, www.roberthalflegal.com
- Yahoo! HotJobs, www.hotjobs.yahoo.com

Information About Legal Employers and Legal Careers

- The American Lawyer's AmLaw 100, www.law.com/jsp/tal/index.jsp

- Avery Index Law Firm Rankings and Information, www.averyindex.com/

- National Association for Legal Career Professionals, www.nalp.org

- Vault.com, www.vault.com

Practical Information About Getting Started in Law Practice

- ABA Practice Areas and Interests, www.abanet.org/membergroups.html

- ABA Risk Management and Professional Liability, www.abanet.org/legalservices/lpl/preventionlibrary.html

- Law Practice Management, www.abanet.org/lpm/home.shtml

- Legal Technology Resource Center, www.abanet.org/tech/ltrc/

Continuing Legal Education and Professional Development

- ABA Center for Continuing Legal Education, www.abanet.org/cle

- Association for Continuing Legal Education, www.aclea.org

- Continuing Legal Education Regulators Association, www.clereg.org/

- DigiLearn Online List of CLE Requirements by State, www.digilearnonline.com/stateReqs.asp

- National Academy of Continuing Legal Education, www.nacle.com/

- Practising Law Institute, http://www.pli.edu/

- West LegalEd Center, http://westlegaledcenter.com/home/homepage.jsf

Networking and Professional Associations for Young Lawyers

- American Bar Association Young Lawyers Division, www.abanet.org/yld/

- Practice Area/Specialty Bar Association Information, www.abanet.org/lawyer.html

- State and Local Bar Association Information, www.abanet.org/barserv/stlobar.html

Work-Life Balance and Maintaining Your Health and Sanity

- ABA Commission on Lawyer Assistance Programs, www.abanet.org/legalservices/colap/

- ABA Standing Committee on Substance Abuse, www.abanet.org/subabuse/home.html

- Building a Better Legal Profession, www.betterlegalprofession.org

- Lawyers' Life Coach, www.lawyerslifecoach.com

Note also that many states have a Lawyers Helping Lawyers or Lawyers Concerned for Lawyers organization, which can help you overcome issues with substance abuse, depression, and stress. Your firm or your law school's student services office should also have referrals to outside counselors or providers.

GLOSSARY

Associates: Attorneys employed at a law firm. Senior associates are attorneys who have not yet been promoted to partnership but have been at the firm for a set number of years; junior associates are young lawyers like you who have been working at the firm for a limited number of years.

Billable hours: Time spent on activities that may be billed out to clients. Billable hour quotas set out the number of hours that you will be expected to bill during a given time period.

Business development: The process of establishing relationships with new clients or expanding relationships with current clients.

Call-back interviews: A subsequent round of interviews after the initial on-campus interview that allows the employer to get to know potential hires better. (*See also* on-campus interviews.)

Career plan: A plan that you can put into action to help you find that all-important first position.

Cover letter: A formal letter to a potential employer that accompanies your resume when you are applying for a position or asking to be considered for future positions.

Ethics: Codes of conduct by which members of a profession are expected to abide.

Evaluation: A process that allows an employer to gauge an employee's performance at the firm and the value the employee brings to the firm.

Firm hierarchies: Well-defined structures and well-defined roles for attorneys at each "lock-step" within the firm's structure.

First-year associate: A lawyer who's fresh out of law school and in his or her first year on the job.

Informational interview: An informal interview or meeting with an experienced attorney during which you seek to find out information about working in the attorney's field or practice area.

Interviews: A formal meeting process that many law firms follow when considering potential applicants.

Job application: A formal document that allows you to apply for a job opening and asks you numerous personal and professional questions.

Marketability: The informal measure of how appealing your skill set, experience, abilities, and contacts may be to a potential employer.

Mentoring: Under formal mentoring programs, new lawyers are assigned to a more seasoned attorney, who may serve several functions: oversee the new lawyer's work product; answer questions; offer ongoing guidance on substantive tasks and other parts of law firm life; provide ongoing training and support to the new attorney; and evaluate the new attorney's work, conduct, and performance for purposes of promotions, compensation, and performance appraisals. In informal mentoring, a seasoned lawyer may simply provide guidance, help, and assistance to the new lawyer.

Networking: The process of establishing, building, and maintaining quality professional relationships.

Non-legal careers: Career paths in which a lawyer does not practice law but uses his or her law degree outside of the legal field.

Nontraditional legal careers: Career paths in which a lawyer does not practice law but uses his or her law degree in a position that involves the legal field.

On-campus interviews (OCI): The interview process by which large law firms quickly interview many candidates for their summer associate and first-year associate positions.

Organizational skills: A set of skills allowing you to effectively organize your work, your resources, and your life, thereby increasing your efficiency and productivity on the job.

Partners: Attorneys who have been promoted to partnership and have been working at the firm for a set number of years. A managing partner may oversee and manage the firm's operations and business.

Practical choices: The multiple decisions you'll have to make regarding practical and technical concerns in your career, including your salary, location, commute, work schedule, and the like.

Practice area: An area of law or broad subject in which lawyers specialize.

Practice group: A department at a law firm (most typically large firms) in which lawyers work in a particular practice area.

Pro bono work: Performing free or low-cost services for clients who can't afford legal representation.

Professional development: Continuing legal education courses and other educational opportunities where you may learn substantive law or practical tips that will help you on the job. In addition, you'll network with other professionals.

Professional image: Exuding professionalism in person, in writing, and online.

Professional or trade associations: Membership groups centered around professionals that allow members to keep up with news and trends in their profession, get the chance to attend continuing legal education and professional and social events, meet others in their field, and get the opportunity to network. Plus, many professional associations maintain their own job boards, job listings, and other career resources for members.

References: Other people's impressions of you as a professional, which can play an important part in determining whether you have the skill set needed for the job and whether you will be a good fit for the firm.

Resume: A formal document that details your education, experience, skills, and overall qualifications for a position.

Self-assessment: A tool to determine your preferences, skills, aptitudes, needs, and goals and other considerations that matter to you.

Solo practice: Self-employment during which an attorney practices law alone at his or her own law firm.

Starter job: Your first position out of law school. A starter job doesn't have to be perfect as long as you're using the job to advance your career and build valuable legal experience that you can take with you on your career journey.

Summer associate positions: Summer-long positions (paid or unpaid, depending on the firm) that allow law students to gain valuable practical experience.

Support staff: Non-attorney legal staff, including paralegals, legal assistants, legal administrators, and others.

Work environment: The many different fields, settings, and positions in which new lawyers may find themselves.

Work-life balance: Achieving a ratio of work to non-work activity that keeps you happy on and off the job.

Workplace diversity: More than adequate representation of ethnicities, this is an all-encompassing cultural issue that includes gender, sexual orientation, socioeconomic status, and life experiences in general.

Writing sample: A formal document that allows a potential employer to gauge your analytical and writing skills, provides a glimpse into the kind and quality of work product you may turn out at the job, presents the employer with an idea of your professional writing style, and allows you to showcase some of your knowledge on a legal issue or topic.

Young lawyers: Typically includes new lawyers who are less than five years out of law school or lawyers under the age of 35. In some contexts, may be referred to as "recent law graduates."

INDEX

A

abilities, displaying, 141–145
advertising, self-employment
  feasibility, 49–50
alternative dispute resolution Web resources, 40
American Bar Association
  (ABA) Web sites
  continuing education/
    professional
    development, 247
  government/public service
    career paths, 53
  job search, 245
  lawyer assistance
    programs, 223, 248
  networking and profes-
    sional associations, 247
  practical information, 246
  technology, 191–193
assignments
  beginning, 162
  flexibility for, 230–231

receiving and dealing
  with, 139–141
showing abilities, 141–145
taking on additional,
  141–144
assistance programs,
  222–224, 248
associates, 249. *See also*
  co-workers
  first-year associates, 250
  summer associate
    positions, 33, 253

B

background checks, 89
banking management
  practice groups, 35
bar admissions in resumes,
  81
big picture of your place in
  firm, 230, 233
billable hours, 249

billing time, 165–166
  organizational system, 184
blogging, 97
  professional image,
    99–103
book of business, 156
  building, 154–156
boutique firms, 37
budgets
  money management,
    188–190
  self-employment
    feasibility, 45–47
burnout
  avoiding, 234
  ethics and professionalism,
    202
  lawyer assistance
    programs, 222–224
  recognizing signs of,
    217–220
business aspects of law
  self-employment
    feasibility, 42–47
  Web resources, 38–39
business cards, networking
  with, 172
business development, 249
  building book of business,
    154–156
  self-employment
    feasibility, 48–49
  tips, 156–158
business skills development,
  127

C

call-back interviews,
  111–112, 249
career development, 127
career fit
  ethics and
    professionalism, 203
  "right fit" factors, 7–10
career journals, 147–148
career paths
  career options, 54–56
  choice considerations, 3–7
  changing directions,
    240–243
  firsthand accounts, 56–58
  government/public
    service, 53–54
  legal, Web sites, 246
career plans, 249
  preparing for second job,
    237–240
  "right fit" factors, 7–10
  sample, 27–29
  worksheet for designing,
    22–26
career sound bites, 98–99
careers
  non-legal careers, 251
  nontraditional legal
    careers, 55, 251
civility, interacting with
  peers, 211–212
client base
  building book of business,
    154–156
  interacting with, 208–209,
    232

making employer market-
able to, 151–153, 234
making yourself market-
able to, 151–153, 232
networking, 171–175, 177
self-confidence with,
156–157
self-employment
feasibility, 48–49
understanding clients'
needs, 157–158
co-workers
interacting with, 232
participating in work life,
145
treating with respect, 231
cold-calling, targeted, 73
communication skills, 231
computer file organization,
183
conferences on technology,
193
contact database
organization, 184
contact information in
resumes, 80
continuing legal education,
126–127, 247
corporate culture, 231
corporate practice groups,
35
cover letters, 249
job search strategy tips,
71, 74
writing, 83–85
cultural diversity in firms,
204–206

D

decision-makers in firm,
identifying, 144
delegating tasks, 162–163,
187
depression, managing,
221–222
dispute resolution Web
resources, 40
diversity in firms, 204–206
dressing
for interviews, 114
for work, organizational
system, 185

E

e-mail
professional image,
99–103
technology discussion
lists, 192–193
education
continuing legal
education, 126–127, 247
ethics and
professionalism, 201
in resumes, 81
electronic file organization,
183
e-mail file organization, 183
employers. *See also* work
environment
big picture, 233
decision-makers,
identifying, 144
diversity in firms,
204–206

interacting with partners/
superiors, 209–211, 232
large-firm hierarchy,
33–34
legal, Web sites, 246
making marketable to
clients, 151–153, 234
making yourself
marketable to, 229–234
marketing efforts
undertaken by, 153–154
participating in work life,
145
potential
aiming resumes at,
82–83
first meeting, 93–95
job search strategy tips,
70–72
networking with,
175–176
qualities looked for in
candidates, 110–112
questions from during
interviews, 106–107,
111–112
questions to during
interviews, 107–112
"right fit" factors, 9
workplace etiquette,
206–208
enthusiasm
during interviews, 110,
115
showing for work,
142–143, 233

ethics, 197–198, 250
interacting with clients,
208–209
*Model Rules of Professional
Conduct*, 198–199
professionalism, 199–200,
234
"ten commandments",
200–203
ethics education, 127
etiquette, workplace,
206–208
evaluations, 250
regular feedback, 144,
146, 231, 233
show enthusiasm for, 143
types, 145–148
expenses, self-employment
feasibility, 43–47
experience in resumes, 81

F

feedback
regular feedback, 144,
146, 231, 233
self-employment
feasibility, 50–52
filing system organization,
182–183
financial management
practice groups, 35
firm hierarchies, 206–207,
250
first year on the job
potential difficulties,
119–122
training, 122–126
first-year associates, 250

flexibility
  for assignments, 145,
    230–231
  job search strategy tips, 75
follow-up when networking,
  172–174, 176
fonts in resumes, 80
formal evaluations, 145–146
formatting
  cover letters, 85
  resumes, 81–82

G

goals
  realistic for work-life
    balance, 217
  "right fit" factors, 8–9
  self-assessment worksheet,
    15–16
gossip
  online professional image,
    100
  workplace etiquette, 207
government career paths,
  53–54
GPSolo magazine, 192

H

health
  burnout. *See* burnout
  maintaining, 221–222, 248
hobbies in resumes, 81
homework, 30, 65, 78, 91–92,
  104, 116, 137–138,
  149–150, 159–160,
  166–167, 178–179,
  194–195, 213, 226, 235, 244

I

illegal activity. *See* ethics
image. *See* professional image
informal training, 124–126
informational interviews,
  57–58, 250
initiative, showing, 229
intellectual property practice
  groups, 35
interests
  "right fit" factors, 7
  self-assessment worksheet,
    13–15
interviewers. *See* employers,
  potential
interviews, 250
  call-back interviews,
    111–112, 249
  career sound bites, 98–99
  first meeting, 93–95
  informational interviews,
    57–58, 250
  networking with potential
    employers, 175–176
  on-campus interviews,
    67–68, 105–110, 251
  professional image, 95–97,
    114–115
  questions from potential
    employers, 106–107
  questions to potential
    employers, 107–110
  references, 88
  resumes, 79–83
  small firms, 113
  writing samples, 85–87

J–K

job applications, 89–90, 250
job search
  activities while
    unemployed, 76–77
  billing time, 165–166
  changing careers,
    240–243
  cover letters, 83–85
  job applications, 89–90
  job postings, 68–69
  networking, 69–70
  on-campus interviews,
    67–68
  preparing for second job,
    237–240
  resumes, 79–83
  strategy tips, 70–75,
    242–243
  Web sites, 245
job skills for career changes,
  242
judicial clerkships, 55–56
junior associates, 34
junior partners, 34

L

languages in resumes, 81
large-firm work
  environment, 32–36
Law Practice Magazine, 192
Law Practice Today, 192
lawyer assistance programs,
  222–224, 248
lawyers
  networking with, 175–177
  young lawyers, 253
legal experience in resumes,
  81

legal professionals,
  networking with, 175–177
letters of recommendation,
  87–89
litigation practice groups, 35

M

managing partners, 33
marketability, 250
  making employer
    marketable to clients,
    151–153, 234
  resume as tool, 82
  yourself to clients,
    151–153, 232
  yourself to employer,
    229–234
marketing
  efforts undertaken by
    employer, 153–154
  self-employment
    feasibility, 49–50
memberships in resumes, 81
mentoring, 124–125,
  250–251
mentors
  ethics and
    professionalism, 201
  finding, 129–134, 233
  networking, 171–175
  questions for, 134–136
mistakes, making on the job,
  123–124
*Model Rules of Professional
  Conduct*, 198–199
money management,
  188–190. *See also* budgets

N

needs (practical considerations)
  career changes, 241
  "right fit" factors, 9–10
  self-assessment worksheet, 16–17
  Web sites, 246
networking, 69–70, 75–76, 251
  approaching lawyers and legal professionals, 175–177
  career sound bites, 98–99
  defined, 169–171
  ethics and professionalism, 202
  for career changes, 242
  tips, 171–175, 232
  Web sites, 247
  workplace etiquette, 207–208
non-legal careers, 251
nontraditional legal careers, 55, 251

O

office space organization, 183
on-campus interviews, 67–68, 105–110, 251
online professional image, 99–103
organization. *See also* time management
  honing organizational skills, 181–185, 233
  job search strategy tips, 71
  networking, 173
  organizational skills, 251
  honing, 181–185, 233

P

partners, 251
  interacting with, 209–211, 232
  learning business development from, 157
  thinking like, 158
  senior partners, 33
past-tense verbs in resumes, 81
periodicals on technology, 192
personal life, work-life balance, 215–217
  recognizing signs of burnout, 217–220
political views, online professional image, 101, 103
practical choices, 251. *See also* needs
practice (legal)
  management, lawyer assistance programs, 222–224
  self-employment feasibility, 42–43, 47–48
  Web resources, 39
practice areas, 251
  tracking trends/changes, 157
practice groups, 34–35, 251
present-tense verbs in resumes, 81
pro bono work, 252
  performing, 220–221

Web resources for small firms/solo practitioners, 40–41

productivity
common pitfalls, 161–163
mastering the basics, 232
strengths/weaknesses checklist, 164–165

professional associations, 252
job search strategy tips, 71–72
Web sites, 247

professional contacts, networking, 171–175

professional development, 252
during unemployment, 76–77
ethics and professionalism, 201
job search strategy tips, 72
opportunities, 126–129
self-employment feasibility, 50–52
Web sites, 247

professional image, 252
ethics and professionalism, 201
interviews, 95–97, 114–115
online and via e-mail, 99–103
projecting, 233–234
thinking like partners, 158

professionalism, 199–200, 234
interacting with clients, 208–209
interacting with partners/superiors, 209–211
interacting with peers, 211–212
"ten commandments", 200–203
workplace etiquette, 206–208

projects. See assignments

proofreading
cover letters, 86
writing samples, 86–87

public service
career paths, 53–54
pro bono work, 220–221
Web resources for small firms/solo practitioners, 40–41

publications with job postings, 68–69

Q

questions
for mentors, 134–136
from employers
during call-back interviews, 111–112
during on-campus interviews, 106–107
to employers
during call-back interviews, 111–112
during on-campus interviews, 107–110

R

references, 87–89, 252
relationships, lawyer assistance programs, 222–224
resumes, 252
  job search strategy tips, 71, 74
  writing, 79–83
role models, 210–211

S

schedule, maintaining, 162
second job, preparing for, 237–240
self-assessment, 10–21, 252
self-confidence
  beginning projects, 162
  during interviews, 110, 114
  with clients, 156–157
self-employment. *See also* solo practices
  determining feasibility, 41–52
self-evaluations, 147–148, 233
senior associates, 34
senior partners, 33
skill-based and practical education, 127
skills
  business skills development, 127
  communication skills, 231
  job skills for career changes, 242
  organizational skills, 181–185, 233, 251

in resumes, 81
"right fit" factors, 9
  self-assessment worksheet, 11–13
  social skills development, 127
  technical skills development, 127
  time management skills, 185–188, 233
  transferable skills for career changes, 241
small firms
  interviews, 113
  Web resources, 37–41
  work environment, 36–37
social skills development, 127
solo practices, 252
  determining feasibility, 41–52
  Web resources, 37–41
starter jobs, 252
stress
  burnout. *See* burnout
  dealing with during unemployment, 77, 224–225
  ethics and professionalism, 202
  lawyer assistance programs, 222–224
  managing, 221–225, 248
  online professional image, 100
substance abuse, managing, 221–222, 248
summer associate positions, 33, 253
superiors, interacting with, 209–211, 232

support staff, 34, 253
  treating with respect, 231
support system for work-life
  balance, 217

T

targeted cold-calling, 73
team efforts, supporting, 230
technical skills development,
  127
technology
  money management tools,
    189
  organizational tools,
    183–184
  professional image, online
    and via e-mail, 99–103
  time management tools,
    187
  Web sites, 191–193
Technology eReport, 192
time management. *See also*
  organization
  billing time, 165–166
    organizational system,
      184
  ethics and
    professionalism, 202
  honing management
    skills, 185–188, 233
  productivity, 162
tracking job search details,
  strategy tips, 71
trade associations. *See*
  professional associations
training. *See also* education
  ethics and
    professionalism, 201

first year on the job,
  122–126
transferable skills for career
  changes, 241

U–V

unemployment
  activities during, 76–77
  stress, dealing with during
    unemployment, 224–225
unethical activity. *See* ethics

W–Z

Web sites
  assistance programs
    (work/relationships/
    stress/depression/
    substance abuse),
    222–224, 248
  Center for Law
    Student Ethics and
    Professionalism, 200
  continuing education/
    professional
    development, 247
  firsthand accounts of
    careers, 56–58
  government/public service
    career paths, 53–54
  job postings, 68–69
  job search, 245
  legal employers/careers,
    246
  networking and profes-
    sional associations, 247
  personal, professional
    image, 99–103

practical information, 246

small firm/solo practice resources, 37–41

technology, 191–193

work-life balance, 218–220

work environment, 253. *See also* career paths

choice factors, 58–64

corporate culture, 231

current statistics, 32

interacting with peers, 211–212

large firms, 32–36

learning basics, 232

"right fit" factors, 8

self-assessment worksheet, 18–20

small firms, 36–37

training on the job, 123

work experiencein resumes, 81

work-life balance, 253

burnout, recognizing signs of, 217–220

lawyer assistance programs, 222–224

maintaining, 215–217

pro bono work, 220–221

stress, managing, 221–222, 224–225

Web sites, 248

workload, balancing, 161–162

workplace diversity, 204–206, 253

workplace etiquette, 206–208

worksheets

designing career plan, 22–26

self-assessment, 10–21

self-employment feasibility, 42–52

writing samples, 85–87, 253

young lawyers, 253

LAW SCHOOL
REVEALED

Secrets, Opportunities, and Success!

Exclusive advice from students, deans, professors, and attorneys

- Keys to choosing the right school
- Candid insight on what to expect and how to get ready
- Best ways to study, master legal research, and write great exams
- Proven steps to avoid burnout and find balance
- New options that make the most of your law school experience

Ursula Furi-Perry, JD
Professor and Columnist for *PreLaw* and *The National Jurist*

jist Works
America's Career Publisher

Also by Ursula Furi-Perry: *Law School Revealed*

About the Author

Ursula Furi-Perry, J.D., is a nationally published legal writer, attorney, and adjunct law professor. She is the author of eight books and more than 300 published articles, and she authors the career column for the *National Jurist,* as well as a column profiling recent law grads for the *Jurist* and its sister publication, *PreLaw Magazine.*

Furi-Perry is the Director of Academic Support at the Massachusetts School of Law. She frequently speaks about law school, legal careers, and related topics to colleges and associations.

She received her Juris Doctor magna cum laude, graduating at the top of her law school class.